T0270466

Studentenfriedhof
to Soldatenfriedhof

Studentenfriedhof
to Soldatenfriedhof

A History of Langemark
German cemetery and
self-guided tour

Roger Steward
Foreword by Dominiek Dendooven

UNIFORM

This book is dedicated to:

*The men and women of all sides who fought and died
in the Ypres Salient during the Great War, and to all my
fellow tour guides who help keep their memory alive.*

Published by Uniform
an imprint of Unicorn Publishing Group
5 Newburgh Street, London
W1F 7RG
www.unicornpublishing.org

All rights reserved. It is not legal to reproduce, duplicate, or transmit
any part of this document in either electronic means or printed format.
Recording of this publication is strictly prohibited.

© Copyright 2021 by Roger Steward

This edition first published by Uniform, 2021

A catalogue record for this book is available from the British Library.

ISBN 978-1-913491-67-3

Dimensions are listed as height x width x depth unless otherwise stated.

Designed by Matthew Wilson
Printed in Turkey by FineTone Ltd

CONTENTS

FOREWORD

During a 'classic' battlefield tour in the Ypres Salient, Tyne Cot cemetery in Passchendaele and the German cemetery in Langemark are usually visited in quick succession. The visitor is not only impressed by the large numbers buried in both places, but is also fascinated by the contrast between the two cemeteries. But unlike Tyne Cot for the British, Langemark is not the largest German military cemetery, not even the largest in the vicinity of Ypres (for that is the much less frequently visited 'Deutsche Soldatenfriedhof Menen', only 25km away). Although the large number of burials in the cemetery in Langemark is sobering and highly relevant, its historical significance lies elsewhere.

Passchendaele and Langemarck – as the place names were written in the old spelling – are to this day names that ring a bell with the heirs of the respective British and German empires. But whereas Passchendaele, as a place of remembrance, is more consecrated than contested, the reverse is true of Langemarck: since the Second World War, Langemarck has increasingly been deliberately forgotten in Germany. This has everything to do with the political role that 'remembering Langemarck' played in Nazi Germany. After all, Langemarck was a symbol of the willingness of German youth to sacrifice their lives for the Fatherland. The way in which the cemetery was laid out in the 1930s was intended to support that discourse, and Langemarck became one of the holy places of National Socialist Germany. After that 'other war' the nationalistic aura disappeared to some extent, but Langemarck's heavily charged past could never be entirely renounced.

The German cemetery in Langemark, much more than any other war site near Ypres, is a historically charged place that needs nuance and interpretation. Those who really want to understand this place must peel it like an onion and strip it of one historical layer after another. That requires a thorough knowledge of the location and the contexts involved: what happened here in 1914? In 1917? In the 1920s? In the 1930s? During the Second World War? In the 1950s, 1980s and during the recent centenary? In short: what made the German military cemetery in Langemark the place it is today?

And it is precisely this much-needed historical work that the author has undertaken by writing this book. For decades, the number of English-speaking visitors to Langemark's German military cemetery has been manyfold the number of German-speaking visitors. And yet until now no English-language book has been available about what is arguably the most important German war site in the Ypres Salient. Roger Steward must be praised for having finally succeeded in writing a much needed addition to the existing English literature on Ypres and its Salient.

Dr Dominiek Dendooven
In Flanders Fields Museum

INTRODUCTION

Very little has been written about Langemark German cemetery with the consideration of the English-speaking visitor. The centenary period of 2014 to 2018 saw approximately 1.1 million visitors to Langemark German cemetery, of which roughly 42 per cent were native English speakers. Second only to Tyne Cot in terms of cemetery visitor numbers, Langemark German cemetery has seen a massive increase in interest and footfall in recent years. English speakers make up the majority of the visitors to the cemetery. Practically every visiting British school group will have Langemark on its agenda, as do the numerous battlefield tour companies and the individual visitors from the modern-day Commonwealth. So why are there so many British and Commonwealth visitors to Langemark? The answer is simple, because they feel (correctly) that it is the right thing to do, the concept of remembrance and respect is built into the psyche of the British and Commonwealth visitor. The idea that the German soldier and the British and Commonwealth soldier were very alike is a common perception voiced by visitors. A distinction is often made between the First World War German soldiers and Second World War German soldiers, the perception being that both wars were very different: First World War German soldiers are viewed as victims whilst Second World War German soldiers are viewed as antagonists. Historical publications and modern-day media have all helped soften the bitterness caused by the two world wars, from the black humour of the *Wipers Times* during the First World War to modern-day TV comedies such as *'Allo 'Allo*, *Black Adder Goes Forth*,

Dad's Army, and *Fawlty Towers* (don't mention the war), all have helped to blunt the edge of post-war mistrust and hatred. Serious literature has also played its part, Erich Maria Remarque's *All Quiet on the Western Front* is the iconic anti-war novel written by, and from the viewpoint of, a German soldier. The book reinforces the perception that the German experience on the Western Front was no different to the British experience, both thought of as victims of war and both subject to the often inaccurate 'lions led by donkeys' syndrome. These perceptions have made the Commonwealth visitor feel that they almost have to visit a German burial ground during their tour of the Ypres Salient.

Although increasing slowly, there are very few German visitors to the Ypres Salient. During the centenary period roughly only 1 per cent of visitors to Langemark German cemetery came from Germany. The sentiment of collective guilt from the German side is subsiding and the few visitors from Germany who do come to the Ypres Salient are more than happy to discuss both wars. This is very much a generational thing, younger Germans are more than happy to talk in detail, older Germans less so. The lack of German visitor numbers can simply be explained by a lack of education about the Great War. The German educational focus is on the Second World War, therefore the history of the First World War often gets overlooked, the few Germans who do have an interest in the Great War tend to visit the French city of Verdun. Verdun represents to the Germans what Passchendaele and the Somme represent to the British.

Due to the lack of published material in the English language, for British and Commonwealth tourists, Langemark German cemetery has become a place of myth and legend, a place where opinions and views have translated into pseudo facts. Some stories have come into being through hearsay, family stories, misinformation or poor research. Many stories evolved post Second World War and were motivated politically and by a dislike of all things German. The occupation of Belgium during the Second World War was the second German occupation in living memory and of course resulted in a strong anti-German sentiment amongst some of the population post-war. This depth of feeling was to have a direct impact on the evolution of the the First World War German grave sites in Belgium during the 1950s.

A visit to Langemark German cemetery is an unforgettable experience. The scale of the burials, the heavy atmosphere and level of upkeep all add to the sadness and empathy felt towards the 44,000 souls who lay in its grounds. The emotional impact of the cemetery triggers many questions and comments from its visitors, many of which I will address in the forthcoming chapters.

The aim of this book is not to promote modern-day political correctness, or to revise history but to tell the story of Langemark German cemetery factually and without bias or judgement. The past is the past, what happened, happened. I leave it to you whether you agree or disagree with the motivations of the time. All I hope is that you find this book informative and that I can dispel a few of the myths and legends surrounding Langemark German cemetery and help you understand its evolution process.

I have split the book into three sections, the first section concentrates on the history of the cemetery and its evolution. The second section of the book is a detailed walking tour of the cemetery explaining each point of interest clearly and concisely, whilst the third section outlines some essential facts and figures. Having read the first half of the book you (the reader) will have a clearer understanding of how Langemark German cemetery evolved from the Studentenfriedhof of the 1930s to the Soldatenfriedhof in later years.

I hope you enjoy my efforts.

Roger Steward
Ypres Battlefield Tours

PART 1:
EVOLUTION

Group of three basalt crosses.

The death toll across all sides during the First World War was on an unprecedented scale. Death had become a common sight for the soldiers of the Ypres Salient. Bodies laid in the battlefields not just for days and months, but for years in many cases. As the front lines stagnated little

movement was possible, the corpses rotted on the battlefield, the dead remained where they had fallen until they were obliterated by the artillery or swallowed by the mud and filth. The situation started to become a major problem for the protagonists. It lowered morale, increased the risk of disease and infection and created an unbearable stench which, at the height of summer, was often detectable miles from the fighting. On the front line, unofficial local truces were organised between the opposing sides, uneasy truces that lasted for a few hours to collect the wounded and bury the dead. Shell holes, mine craters and disused trenches were all utilised as makeshift graves, sometimes as communal graves containing the remains of both friend and foe, enemies in life but comrades in death, inseparable for eternity. If possible, a makeshift grave marker identifying the burials would be erected, however, many of these grave markers and grave sites would be destroyed by the relentless artillery fire that combed the battlefields making no distinction between the dead and the living. Behind the front lines, a more structured story emerged, organised burial sites were constructed, often around the sites of dressing stations and hospitals where not all men would survive their wounds. Regimental cemeteries were also common, men from a unit would often bury their comrades together, the same cemeteries would then be used and expanded by other units as they came into the sector and started to incur the inevitable casualties. At the conclusion of the First World War, an estimated 500,000 soldiers of all nationalities had lost

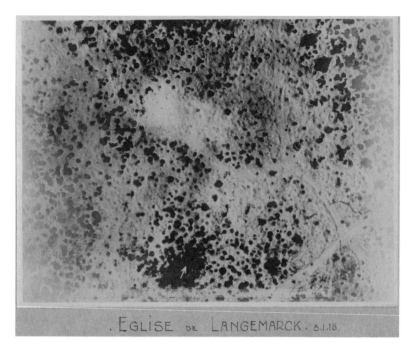

.EGLISE de LANGEMARCK. 5.1.18.

Aerial picture of the battlefields around Langemark taken in 1918.

their lives in the approximate 100 sq. miles of the Ypres Salient. The Ypres Salient had become the graveyard of the armies of the Great War, a war grave on an incomprehensible scale. The burial units would not be short of work.

The German Army layed claim to roughly 210,000 of the grim death toll, 210,000 bodies which had to be located, recorded and reburied so the development of organised and recorded burial grounds was essential. The task of locating, recording and burying the bodies started during the war itself. From as early as 1914 the Germans were using civilian burial grounds such as local churchyards to bury their war dead. As the casualty rate increased, purpose-built military cemeteries were constructed as demand started to outstrip capacity.

In the spring of 1915 after the 2nd Battle of Ypres, aided by the use

of chlorine gas, the Germans had pushed the Allies back nearly 3 miles to the line of the Yser Canal. Once the fighting had settled down, the German burial units set to the task of combing the former battlefields for the bodies of the fallen. For this task, the German Army used its medical units (Sanitatskompanien), labour units (Armierungstruppen) and also Belgian civilians and prisoners of war, the latter monitored by the German Field Police (Feldgendarme). In the summer of 1915, the German 4th Army formed specific military burial units for this task. By the spring of 1917, most of the solitary field graves had been recovered and reburied in the more permanent concentration cemeteries constructed behind the lines.

The creation of German regimental cemeteries in 1914 and 1915 led to a standardisation of design in 1916 and 1917. Regimental cemeteries were, as the name suggests, constructed by members

The reality of an early battlefield burial ground.

of a regiment for the fallen of that regiment, this equated to elaborate cemetery designs containing different types of headstones and monuments, all paid for by fundraising by the regiment, but all of course designed to reflect the honour and the glory of the said regiment. In 1916, a special committee was set up to develop criteria for the design of the German cemeteries. The Kaiser himself issued an order on 28 February 1917 which stipulated, amongst other things, that the military cemeteries at the front line should be simple in design and harmonius with nature. The idea was to portray the glory of the soldier's death, a sacred and honourable death for the Fatherland. This design theme continued through into later years as you will see regarding Langemark German cemetery. The German burial units also started to record the position and details of graves known, and possible sites of unknown burials, to allow for exhumations and searches at a later date; each sector had a Grave Officer (Gräberoffizer) appointed to complete this ongoing task.

The huge British offensive of 1917 known as the Third Battle of Ypres, resulted in many of the German cemeteries constructed during the years of 1914 to 1917 being laid to waste by almost constant artillery fire. After firing an estimated 4.25 million shells in the space of two weeks the British artillery had devasted the ground behind the German lines. Graves were destroyed, bodies bought to the surface and blown apart. Trenches and defensive positions were sometimes dug through burial sites. Many men's graves were lost forever.

Trooper Harry Kendall of the 1st King Edwards Light Horse (British Army) wrote of that period:

'I was stationed for some time on these crossroads near the Essex Farm graveyard. Fritz had a bad habit of sending shells over and ploughing up the graves. For many weeks there was little peace at that end of Essex Farm road – even for the glorious dead. Often a dozen times a day we were smothered over with mud from the graves torn up by Fritz's exhuming shells. Possibly the worst phase of this post by number four bridge was the eternal reviewing of the dead men before one's tiring eyes. Slaughtered men lying about in all shapes and forms around this unholy post of ours. Sometimes these immolated human beings would be wrapped in army blankets, tied around the head and feet. At other times, nothing but War's frightful disfigurement or mutilations were to be seen on the faces of these "glorious corpses".'

Early German burials.

The same ground was fought over again in the spring of 1918 when the Germans launched their great spring offensive, when they advanced almost to the gates of Ypres, and then again towards the end of that year, when the Allies regained the lost ground and finally broke out of the Ypres Salient. The German Army retreated, leaving its cemeteries and its fallen behind.

At the end of the First World War, there were c.200 German burial grounds spread across the municipalities and districts of Belgium plus thousands of field graves and unrecovered bodies that still lay in the battlefields. These bodies had to be recovered, documented and then reburied, a massive logistical task, one that would require cooperation, organisation and ultimately reconciliation. The big problem for the Germans now was how was this to be achieved.

Signed in 1919, the Treaty of Versailles not only concerned itself with imposing reparations on Germany but covered many other issues which needed to be resolved, one of those being the management of the burials and grave sites of the fallen. Cemeteries, field graves and unrecovered bodies were scattered across the Ypres Salient, the same picture being reflected in France and all the other theatres of war around the world. Legislation needed to be put into place to organise and manage the massive logistical task of caring for the fallen. The Treaty of Versailles went some way in trying to afford a solution to this problem.

Articles 225 and 226 concerned the creation and upkeep of the graves:

Treaty of Versailles

SECTION II.

GRAVES.

ARTICLE 225.

The Allied and Associated Governments and the German Government will cause to be respected and maintained the graves of the soldiers and sailors buried in their respective territories.

They agree to recognise any Commission appointed by an Allied or Associated Government for the purpose of identifying, registering, caring for or erecting suitable memorials over the said graves and to facilitate the discharge of its duties.

Furthermore they agree to afford, so far as the provisions of their laws and the requirements of public health allow, every facility for giving effect to requests that the bodies of their soldiers and sailors may be transferred to their own country.

ARTICLE 226.

The graves of prisoners of war and interned civilians who are nationals of the different belligerent States and have died in captivity shall be properly maintained in accordance with Article 225 of the present Treaty.

The Allied and Associated Governments on the one part and the German Government on the other part reciprocally undertake also to furnish to each other:

(1) A complete list of those who have died, together with all information useful for identification.

(2) All information as to the number and position of the graves of all those who have been buried without identification.

The first paragraph of article 225 passed the responsibility for the upkeep of war graves onto the owner of the territories where the bodies were interred. The potential ramifications for Belgium were huge, as over 500,000 dead lay on its soil. The reality on the ground was somewhat different as the Allies already had their plans in place, plans to make the cemeteries a fitting resting place for their fallen who had sacrificed everything in the name of freedom. Britain thought of Ypres as holy ground, its ground. Winston Churchill had petitioned for Ypres to be left as a ruin to commemorate the dogged defence of the Salient by the British Army. The British standpoint was that the immortal Salient was the property of the Empire as so much British blood had been spilt in its defence. To reinforce this, British and Commonwealth memorials were placed at significant sites immediately after the war, some had permission, some not but all remained in situ. In short, the victors left their mark all over the Salient. Numerous British cemeteries had been established on foreign battlefields during the war. The then Imperial War Graves Commission (IWGC) under the guidance of Sir Fabian Ware was set up to manage these cemeteries. After much discussion and debate at parliamentary level, the British had decided at an early stage against repatriating their dead, leaving large numbers of British dead in cemeteries, both existing and new, on Belgian territory. In terms of design, they were to become a very conscious statement, one that reflected the nation's need to mourn its dead in a manner acceptable to the families denied the chance to repatriate the remains of their loved ones. As a result, an agreement was reached between the British and Belgian governments which allowed the British and Commonwealth via the IWGC to be responsible for maintaining its war graves both financially and logistically. This gave the British and Commonwealth control of the design and level of upkeep of their cemeteries. The Belgian government was more than happy to expropriate and then donate the land to the British and Commonwealth provided the land was used for military burials. From a Belgian perspective, the agreement served a dual purpose, the first and main was to show gratitude for the sacrifice the British Empire had made in the defence of Belgium, the second was more practical, it relieved the Belgian government from the potential cost and responsibility of maintaining British war graves, a cost it could ill afford after its infrastructure had been ravaged by four years of war. For both parties, this was a win-win situation, a happy partnership as such. With the odd exception, Belgian landowners understood the reasons why some of their land was to be given over to the Allies for its burials, the 'odd exceptions' were not highly thought of by their fellow countrymen![1]

The French policy in the Ypres Salient was a similar story with the exception that French families were given the option to repatriate their dead. The bodies that remained in the depleted French cemeteries were then moved to the French concentration cemetery at St Charles Potijze, or if they were buried in British and Allied cemeteries they remained in situ. To this day there are 9,539 French burials in CWGC cemeteries in Belgium. The responsibility for the care of the German war graves was handed to the Belgians (except for the c.2,500 German graves which remained in the IWGC

cemeteries in Belgium). Financially and logistically Germany was in no position to look after its war dead, nor would it have been welcomed back to do so. The Belgian government was faced with the task of having to locate and organise an estimated 140,000 German graves which lay in over 700 different locations, not including the thousands of unrecovered bodies in the former battlefields. The Ypres Salient saw the worst of the fighting and four years of static trench warfare so the majority of German burials in Belgium were located in Flanders.

In the early 1920s, the task of body recoveries continued, mainly by Allied units formed specifically for this purpose. Due to the huge amount of remains to be recovered, and limited manpower when it came to identifying German remains, some units would be more thorough than others. Many sets of newly recovered German remains were just reburied as quickly as possible as unknown soldiers in the existing and newly created German burial sites. The attitude of the men of the grave exhumation units with regards to the recovery of German remains was very pragmatic, Stephen Graham wrote of a conversation with men of a British exhumation unit near Polygon Wood in the late 1920s:

'You must dig up a fair number of Germans. What do you do with them?'

'Leave them where they are. We notifies the authorities, that's all. Of course Jerry

---

1   A good example of this is displayed on an information board at the Ploegsteert Memorial with regards to the moving of Allied burials from the old Rosenberg Military cemetery to Berks Extension cemetery. Whilst stopping short of naming the family the locally produced information board is quite blunt in its description of why the burials had to be moved 'The Rosenberg Chateau plots to its left were moved from their original burial site in the chateau grounds in 1930, the owner refusing permission for their staying there'.

buried most of his own, and I'll give him credit for that, he gave every man his eight feet. You don't so easy come across a man the Germans buried, but some of ours----'

'The weather-beaten Tommy, in old flannel shirt and sagging breeches, waved his hand and grinned with mirth at our British ways 'S a funny thing though-- the British dead keep much longer than the Germans. If I put a spade through something and it's soft, I know it's a Jerry.'

'They say the body of a drunkard keeps fresh longest of all because of the spirit in it.'

'Yes, that's true. And if buried in an oilskin it makes a heap of difference. But it's queer what you find. We came on a fellow the other day with a bayonet through his jaw. He'd been buried that way. No one could get the bayonet out----'

'Aren't the Germans doing anything to keep their dead? The Belgians would look after them if they got a hint from Berlin that it would be worth while.'

'Oh, we'd bury them like Christians if they'd give us another half-crown on our wages. We ain't got nothing agin 'em-- specially the dead.'

By the early 1920s, there were *c.*200 German cemeteries spread across Belgium, the majority being located in Flanders. The maintenance and upkeep of the German cemeteries by the Belgian War Graves Commission (Services des Sépultures Millitaires) was understandably 'bare minimum', damaged stone headstones (erected by Regiments and German families during the war) were taken away and used as foundations for roads and building projects, the original wooden crosses were also removed when they became rotten and were replaced by inferior wooden versions with zinc nameplates provided by the Belgian War Graves Commission. The German graves also came under the regulations of standard Belgian burial law at the time, meaning legally the graves could be disposed of after five years. The Belgians had only granted the Germans the minimal grave concession, something they were about to use as a blunt but effective bargaining tool.

The land arrangements for the German cemeteries in Belgium differed greatly from arrangements offered to the British and French for their cemeteries. The Belgian government had expropriated and then donated the use of the land to the British and French in perpetuity, the land for the German cemeteries was not expropriated by the state and so the landowners on whose land the German cemeteries were now sited received no compensation for the loss of the use of their land, causing deep resentment. As the cemeteries slowly deteriorated under Belgian care, the landowners would sometimes remove fences from the German grave sites to allow cattle and pigs to roam and feed amongst the burial crosses. Sometimes unsanctioned building work encroached onto a cemetery's territory, there was even a case of land being put up for sale with a German cemetery included. Most of the infringements went unpunished but they were to have an impact.

As early as 1919/1920 British veterans and their families started to visit the Western Front to visit the graves of their loved ones. Some simply came to visit the sites which they had read so much about in the British press, to walk through a trench, to clamber over

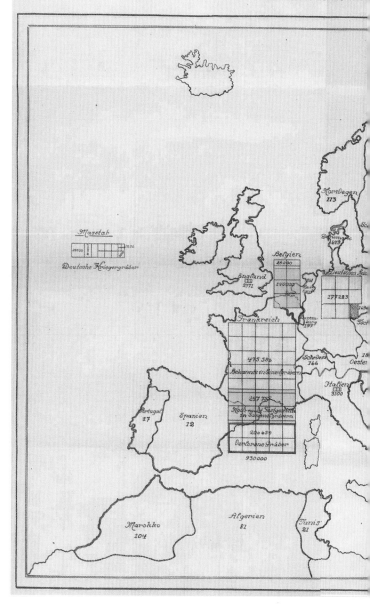

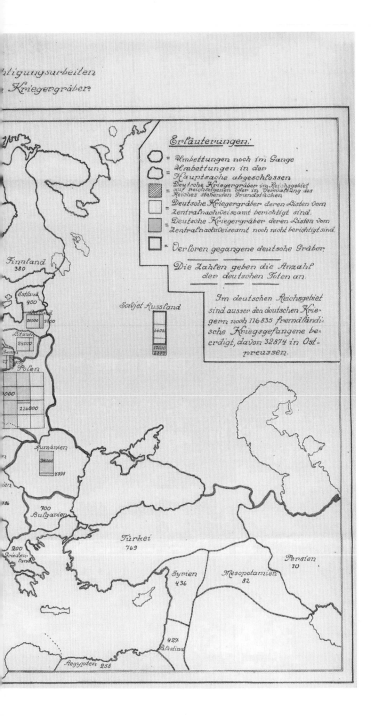

...tigungsarbeiten
...Kriegergräber

Erläuterungen:

◯ = Umbettungen noch im Gange
◯ = Umbettungen in der Hauptsache abgeschlossen
▨ = Deutsche Kriegergräber im Reichsgebiet auf reichseigenen oder in Verwaltung des Reiches stehenden Grundstücken
☐ = Deutsche Kriegergräber deren Listen vom Zentralnachweiseamt berichtigt sind
☐ = Deutsche Kriegergräber deren Listen vom Zentralnachweiseamt noch nicht berichtigt sind
☐ = Verloren gegangene deutsche Gräber

Die Zahlen geben die Anzahl der deutschen Toten an.

Im deutschen Reichsgebiet sind ausser den deutschen Kriegern noch 116835 fremdländische Kriegsgefangene beerdigt, davon 32874 in Ostpreussen.

Finnland
380

Estland
400

...land
21000 3000

Litauen
24000

Polen

...000

116000

Sowjet Russland

36700

17000
1390

Rumänien
36000
2398

...en
...84

700
Bulgarien

200
Griechenland

Türkei
769

Syrien
436

Mesopotamien
82

Persien
10

427
Palastina

Aegypten 258

the rusting hulk of a tank and maybe find a souvenir or two to take home. The Germans also started to return to the Salient, their motivation being more of a pilgrimage than a sightseeing tour. For some, it was a visit of sadness and remembrance, but for others (as a result of National Socialist propaganda in the 1930s) they wished to visit the sites where the 'German heroes lay', the German youth who had 'willingly' sacrificed their lives for the Fatherland, the German youth whose spirits had now risen to a higher plain of Valkyrian myth. Their belt buckles had read 'Gott Mit Uns', (God with us), 210,000 of their sons remained in Flanders Fields.

The reality and logistics of their visits were somewhat less symbolic and glamorous, they were advised to travel in groups and to keep a low profile, they were the invader during the First World War and a losing one at that. The situation that confronted the German pilgrims in the Ypres Salient was one which was not to their liking. All over the Salient, the Allies had placed monuments at key sites celebrating battles won by the units or countries involved. British cemeteries seemed to be at every corner, each one well-kept and a fitting resting place for the soldiers buried in their grounds. Where were the German monuments they asked? On visiting their own cemeteries, they found them to be in an unacceptable condition. They returned home upset and angry.

The Volksbund Deutsche Kriegsgräberfürsorge (VDK), a non-governmental charity based organisation and one of several German war grave organisations at the time, published a magazine entitled the *Kriegsgräberfürsorge* in which the German pilgrims could tell the story of their visits. The stories told were not of a positive nature. Questions started to be asked at higher levels. Something had to be done about the situation.

Initially, the VDK attempted to diffuse the situation by communicating with the aggrieved families and the Belgian War Graves Commission. It was arranged that German families could pay the Belgian War Graves Commission to place flowers and wreaths on graves or to receive a picture of a headstone, a grave could also receive extra care, but all had to be paid for by the families. These arrangements did little to suppress the growing tide of public concern in Germany about the condition of their war graves, particularly when it came to public attention that the German ambassador to Belgium could not compile an official report on the condition of the German cemeteries in Belgium as he was refused access by the Belgian authorities.

The German government had to act, so in 1925 talks began between Belgium and Germany to come to an agreement to resolve the issue. However, Belgium held all of the cards during the negotiations, the German burial sites were on Belgian soil managed by Belgian caretakers, the German government had little influence, particularly when the Belgians threatened to remove the German graves as the five-year grave concession was nearly up. Was the grave concession, the poor level of upkeep and lack of access a conscious ploy by the Belgian government to lessen the burden on itself of maintaining the German burial sites? The more cynical of us may well say yes, the less cynical may argue that fate helped the Belgian hand. Whatever the reason, an agreement was reached and signed in 1926.

The agreement reached seemed to be a good solution for both parties. First of all, the German government agreed to take over responsibility both financially and logistically for the care of all German military cemeteries in Belgium. In return for the Germans relieving the Belgians of their legal responsibility, under Article 225 of the Treaty of Versailles, the Belgian government agreed to officially expropriate the ground for the German cemeteries and hand it over to the Germans provided it was used for military burials only, thus giving the Germans the same rights as the Allies as dictated by the agreement. To help appease the Belgian landowners and to limit the financial costs of both parties it was agreed to reduce the number of German burial sites from 184 to 170. The Belgian government agreed to pay for the exhumation costs and transportation of the bodies to the remaining cemeteries. The reduction in the number of cemeteries was completed by 1934. The land then being given back to its owners. The agreement of 1926 was kept confidential, as from a Belgian perspective, it breached Article 225 of the Treaty of Versailles, and from a German perspective, the idea of other countries finding out that the Germans were paying for the upkeep of their cemeteries in Belgium was not a happy one, as it could lead to similar claims from other countries such as France who had many German cemeteries on its territory.

The new agreement was to impact directly on the remaining German cemeteries, especially Langemark Nord, the cemetery which would soon evolve into the Studentenfriedhof.

Section of German map detailing an estimated overview of German burials in Belgium, France and England'.

Design Policy

From as early as 1917 the German authorities had introduced design guidelines for their military cemeteries. Kaiser Wilhelm II had dictated that the cemeteries should be of a simple design which would reflect the regimental demeanor of the soldier. The ethos of esprit de corps was paramount, the cemeteries were to be communal burial areas, comrades laying side by side in graves marked by plain crosses which were to be identified by reference numbers only. No distinction would be made by rank or religious denomination, no man was to be subordinate to another as all had answered his country's call and all had sacrificed their lives for the Fatherland. The theme of nature also played an important role in the early design principles; the cemeteries would be integrated into their immediate surroundings to create an aura of peace and harmony to take the mind away from the reality of mass violent death. The German burial grounds were to be sacred places and, as such, the overall desire was to create a piece of *Heimat* for their fallen heroes; a piece of Germany in a foreign land.

As the war progressed several designers came and went but by the end of the war most of the original design principles were still in place:

1. The cemetery grounds would be separated from its surroundings by a moat or a low wall to emphasise the sacrosanct nature of its grounds.

2. The cemetery would be integrated into the landscape, the boundary walls kept low so the surroundings could

be easily viewed from the cemetery, harmonising it with the adjacent countryside.

3. Trees, in particular oak trees were to be planted in the cemeteries to symbolise the natural process of life and death and the returning of the body to mother earth.

The use of the oak was a conscious decision, the oak being a national symbol of Germany and had been since well before the First World War. To the Germans, the mighty oak was a symbol of strength and endurance and over the centuries oak groves had become spiritual places of myth and legend. The idea of planting an oak grove was followed through in the post-war design in Langemark in the late 1920s.

4. Natural materials were to be used and the skills of artisan were to be employed in the construction of the cemeteries. The use of concrete was rejected with Germanic rock preferred, such as Weser sandstone or basalt.

5. The horticultural planting scheme in the cemetery would integrate the cemetery into its surroundings. Nothing flamboyant or bombastic would be accepted. Hornbeam hedging, heathers, oak and lime trees were all to be widely used.

6. Oak crosses or oak grave markers were to be used to mark the graves; concrete was not to be considered. The crosses were to be marked with plot numbers, not with names or ranks, the aim being to highlight the camaraderie of the fallen.

7. The entrance to the cemetery should be simple and dignified, not imperialistic or militaristic.

8. Next to the entrance, a Listenraum (List Room) should be constructed where the records of the fallen interred in the cemetery where to be kept.

9. Inscriptions, sculptures and pictures could be placed to enhance the design principles.

10. Budget requirements must be adhered to.

Because of the economic hardship Germany was enduring at the time, the construction and designs of the cemeteries had to be cost-effective but without giving the impression that the honouring of the war dead was subject to financial constraints.

All of these design principles were still being used after the war, but in Langemark's case they were also to take on a strong nationalist theme in the 1930s.

The history of the German organisations responsible for the upkeep and management of their war graves is surprisingly fragmented in the early days of their conception, mainly due to external factors and financial restraints. During the First World War, the management of German grave sites was the responsibility of the German Army and the units it created for this process. By 1917 the system was so advanced that well-known designers were being consulted on cemetery design. However, by the end of the war, many cemeteries had been destroyed by the ebb and flow of the fighting and most of the records the Germans had so carefully documented had been lost or destroyed. As dictated by the Treaty of Versailles, the responsibility for the care of the German war graves in Belgium was imposed on the Belgian state after the war, but when the responsibility was handed back to the Germans after the Belgian/German agreement of 1926, the German government needed to raise an organisation or organisations to manage their cemeteries in Belgium. During the period of Belgian control, the German cemeteries had fallen into poor condition, a fact highlighted to the German government by returning pilgrims who had visited Belgium to see the graves of their loved ones. As a result, several organisations were formed in Germany to improve the care of their war graves. The highest profile of these organisations was the Volksbund Deutsche Kriegsgräberfürsorge (VDK). Formed in 1919 and funded by donations it soon absorbed the other organisations. In addition to the VDK the German government formed the Amtliche Deutsche Graberdienst (ADG), the official German war graves commission. It was agreed that the ADG would be responsible for all the German cemeteries in Belgium, except for two: those at Roeselare and Langemark Nord. These were to be handed over to the care of the VDK making them responsible for the upkeep and redesign of these cemeteries. The head designer of the VDK Robert Tischler started to draw up new design plans for the German cemetery at Langemark, known at the time as Langemark Nord. There was one factor which would dominate the funding, renaming and the redesign of Langemark Nord, that factor being the infamous Langemark myth, known to the Germans at the time as the *Kindermord*.

The Kindermord

During and after the First World War the name Langemark became of huge significance to the Germans. It would come to symbolise the loss of German youth, German heroes laying down their lives in sacrifice for the Fatherland. This 'Massacre of the Innocents' evolved into a glorification of death and a celebration of the camaraderie of the young German soldiers. It would also become the propaganda tool of a regime that used the politicisation of the fallen to its full advantage. The First Battle of Ypres was fought between 15 October and 24 November 1914. During this period both sides suffered staggering losses on the battlefields surrounding Ypres. Official German records claim approximately 134,000 casualties of which 19,600 were killed, the British, French and Belgian figures were as equally devastating. The French are reported to have incurred between 50,000 to 85,000 casualties, the Belgians suffered approximately 18,500 casualties and the British 58,155 casualties including 7,960 killed. In some British battalions, there was only one officer and barely 30 men left when the First Battle of Ypres concluded. Famously Major General E.S. Bulfin of the 2nd Infantry Brigade of the British Expeditionary Force (BEF) claimed of this period, 'We were only clinging to the ground by our eyelids'. Things were equally bad on the German side, for example, Adolf Hitler's unit the 16th Bavarian Reserve Infantry Regiment (BRIR 16) started the 1st Battle of Ypres with about 3,600 men and ended up with only 611. Within those figures, the company in which Hitler served had started with 250 men and ended with only 42.

On 11 November 1914, an official communique from the German Army leadership announced that 'young regiments' west of Langemark had conquered enemy lines whilst singing *Deutschland über alles* as they advanced. The 'young regiments' were newly formed regiments of volunteers, originating from the university cities of Germany and their ranks containing a proportion of scholars and boys of university age. After receiving little training they were rushed to the front and thrown into battle. The rest is history, the tight-knit ranks of the young German volunteers were decimated by the professional soldiers of the British and French armies, It is believed that anything up to 3,000 young Germans were lost. That morning almost all German newspapers ran this as their front page story. However, in an attempt to avoid a propaganda disaster, no mention was made of the disastrous losses and the military failure. The newspapers depicted a scene of glory, the cream of German youth advancing in waves with arms linked, singing patriotic songs and stepping over the bodies of their fallen comrades, each one ready to die

a hero's death for the Fatherland. The myth of the *Kindermord* was born.

The reality of the *Kindermord* was very different to the one portrayed by the German media, the account of German units singing *Deutschland über alles* may be partly true, the song was not adopted as the official German anthem until 1922, but there are reports of Germans singing as they advanced in other areas, some historians claim songs were sung to identify units concealed by the smoke of gunfire on the battlefield, others claim it may have been to bolster spirits and boost adrenalin as they advanced towards the enemies lines. Did they advance arm in arm? I would suggest not, they were fully armed soldiers and would have needed both hands available to fire their weapons. The reality is most of them would have been terrified, their first time in battle facing an onslaught they could not have anticipated and every one of them desperate to avoid a 'hero's' death'. The German communique of 11 November describes the action as taking place 'West of Langemark' the actual location

Right: The Kindermord.

Below: German soldiers advancing across the battlefield.

LANGEMARCK — 1914

being on the outskirts of the Flemish village of Bixschoote. The German press, however, quickly linked the action with the town of Langemark, as it had a more Germanic name than Bixschoote particularly when you spelled it in German; Langemarck. There was no major action recorded at Langemark on 10 November certainly not on a scale you could describe as a 'Massacre of the Innocents'. The makeup of the German regiments was also a different story. Approximately 15 per cent were thought to be of student age, the rest being made up of men from all ages and different backgrounds. The *Kindermord* was far from being so.

Whilst the official narrative of the Kindermord linked it specifically to the actions of 10 November 1914, many other actions took place around the Langemark area during the period of late October to early November 1914. On 23 October 1914, the 1st Battalion Gloucestershire Regiment (Glosters) was in action on the site of what was to become Langemark cemetery. The Glosters had dug positions across the road at the entrance of the modern day cemetery, facing away from Langemark village. At 9.00 a.m. the Glosters spotted a large group of German infantry with mounted officers advancing towards them and engaged. The fighting was intense and carried on throughout the day eventually ceasing by 6.00pm. The inexperienced German units had faced the professional and well trained British Army of the day, the BEF, hard experienced soldiers of the British Empire with a high percentage of trained marksmen in its ranks. Each marksman was more than able to fire fifteen aimed rounds at a target of 300yds, or 270m, the so-called 'Mad Minute'. By the end of the action, hundreds of Germans lay

dead in front of the Gloucestershire positions, each British soldier having fired an average of 500 rounds during the day. By the early 1920s, the actions during this period were to be portrayed collectively as 'The Kindermord' by the German student associations who were desperate to link themselves to its perceived glory. The story of the *Kindermord* was to have a profound impact on the design and evolution of Langemark Nord in the 1920s.

The Birth of Langemark Nord: The Studentenfriedhof

The small town of Langemark and its surrounding area changed hands no less than five times during the First World War. The same ground had been fought over time and again, suffering devastating artillery barrages and mass attacks. By the end of the conflict, Langemark was a wasteland. Thousands of unburied bodies and field graves were scattered around the old battlefields and the remnants of at least fifteen large German war time burial grounds remained in the Langemark area.

Langemark Nord was originally formed in October 1914 by two units of the German 4th Army, RIR 234 (Reserve Infantry Regiment 234) and RJG Btl 23 (Reserve Jager Battalion 23). By the end of 1916 there were 1, 107 burials recorded in Langemark Nord but as a result of the fighting of 1917 and 1918 this figure was reduced to 859 burials by the end of the war. Of the 859 remaining burials, 627 of them were German, the balance being a mix of British, Belgian and French. The first design of Langemark Nord was made by German troops in 1914/15, who fenced the cemetery grounds with privet and beech hedges. The burial site was designed as an oak grove, interspersed with beech, linden and maple trees. The graves were marked with wooden crosses, with ornamental shrubs in between. By the time the war was over, Langemark Nord had again reverted to battlefield, most of the design features put in place earlier in the war had become victim of the devastating artillery fire of 1917 and 1918. The cemetery had merged into the desolate landscape, a few scattered graves remained amongst the mud and shell holes.

Langemark Nord at the end of the war. Note what looks like bunkers on the left side boundary of the cemetery.

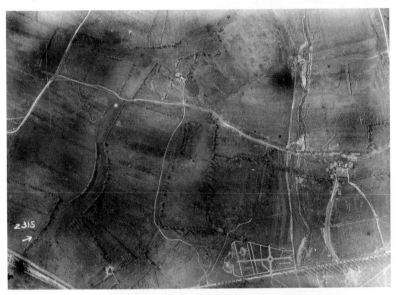

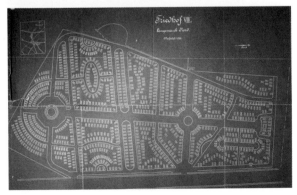

Above: Belgian aerial photograph of Langemark Nord taken on 31 August 1916. Compare it to the original plan.

Right: Early German plan of Langemark Nord.

Between the years of 1919 to 1926 as dictated by the Treaty of Versailles, the German cemeteries were managed by the Belgian War Graves Commission and Langemark Nord fell into disrepair. The big change came in 1926 when the Germans took over control of their cemeteries from the Belgian War Graves Commission as a result of a new Belgian/German war graves agreement.

The metamorphosis from Langemark Nord to the now infamous Studentenfriedhof (students cemetery) has its roots in the 1920s and was firmly

Above: The Inaguration.

Below: Magazine cover of the official magazine of the VDK showing the entrance to Langemark after its inauguration.

LANGEMARCK MCMXIV-MCMXVIII

established in the German psyche by the 1930s. In the 1920s, the myth of the Kindermord was enthusiastically adopted by the powerful German student associations of the time. The Deutsche Studentenschaft, (German Student Union) considered themselves not only to be Germany's elite but also the future of the Reich. By converting the phrase 'young regiments' from the German Army leadership's communiqué of 1914 into the more specific term 'student regiments' they directly connected themselves to the myth of Langemark and were determined to use the myth to its full advantage. In 1928, a delegation from the Deutsche Studentenschaft made a surprise visit to Langemark German cemetery Nord, angered by its state of neglect they returned home to Germany and publicly voiced their outrage. The Langemark Nord, they had found, was an overgrown shell-pitted piece of wasteland, the scattered graves in no order and the burial crosses in poor condition. This was not a fitting place of burial for the heroes of 1914. The public outrage was a propaganda coup for the student associations. They had effectively taken ownership of the Langemark legend and now had the moral ground needed to reconstruct the cemetery to their design principles. In 1928 the student associations launched a charity called the Langemark Donation. Launched on 11 November 1928, fundraising events organised by the student associations took place right across Germany. The purpose of the events was two-fold: to raise funds to construct a cemetery worthy of the student legend and to reinforce the student associations links with the Langemark myth. By the early 1930s enough funds had been raised for the redesign of Langemark Nord to begin.

As a privately funded venture, the student associations were free to make their own choice of designer, bypassing the official German authorities they approached Robert Tischler the head designer of the VDK and commissioned him to design the cemetery. Tischler, like many of the German student associations, had close links with the NSDAP and his political leanings and the requests of the Studentenschaft would heavily influence his design of Langemark. The primary goal of the student associations was not only to create a burial ground fit for the young German heroes of 1914, but also to create a place of pilgrimage for the German youth groups who worshiped the Langemark myth and everything it represented. The Studentenschaft had one other aim, that they were to be interwoven into the fabric of the cemetery. Tischler was happy to oblige.

The cemetery was inaugurated on 10 July 1932. Although the ceremony was subdued the deputy chairman of the VDK made a long speech which was full of reference to the German students and the symbolism of the Kindermord. He stated:

'Only solemn devotion and silent awe should move in here. The massive Weser stones are talking, the young oaks are calling, the red poppies and the all-encompassing watercourse are announcing the once long march. Above all, however, hovers the living spirit of our brothers, we face it in our minds and consciences in order to become aware of the Langemarck, which is more than a building and an event: the Langemarck in spirit. In 1928 Langemark had been merely a word, now it is a sacred site.'

With that phrase, the Studentenfriedhof was born.

Between the years of 1926 to 1932, as a result of the Belgian/German war grave agreement, the number of burials in Langemark Nord had increased dramatically. Several German cemeteries from the local area were concentrated into Langemark Nord, and with the addition of battlefield recoveries, the burial rate swelled to 10,143, of which 3,836 were unidentified.

Robert Tischler's new design of Langemark Nord was influenced by several factors, first and foremost the principles of German cemetery design, the requests of the German student associations and the more practical issue of the huge increase in the number of burials. Much of Tischler's original design remains today with some later alterations and additions. Pre 1932 Tischler had reformed the cemetery into a rectangular plot of 210m length and 90m width which gave it a total area of 18,900sqm. In keeping with the German design principles, Tischler had split the cemetery grounds into two parts – the first an Eichenhain or Oak Grove and on the northern end of the cemetery an elevated second part called the Ehrenfeld or Field of Honour sometimes also referred to as the Mohnfeld or Poppy Field. The Oak Grove was the burial area and was enclosed by a low grass topped wall. The Poppy Field had no burials but had in its grounds three German bunkers and was surrounded by a wall and a moat. On the other side of the wall the cemetery was enclosed on three sides by rows of willows to blend the cemetery into the surrounding landscape.

Above: 1932 cemetery plan.

Opposite: The Wassergrabben showing the original height of the cemetery wall and the Mohnfeld on the other side.

Again, in keeping with the original design principles, the main entrance building was built from red Weser sandstone and measured 13 x 5m. The rough hewn pillars of the narrow entrance led into the gatehouse which had a central passageway and two side rooms. The side room on the right side was known as the Listenraum or List Room or also as the Ehrenraum or Room of Honour. The walls of the room were lined with oak panels. Carved into these panels in alphabetical order

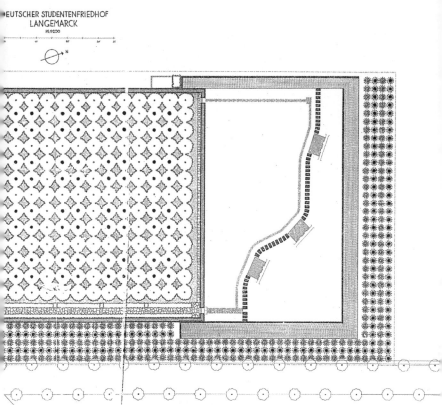

EUTSCHER STUDENTENFRIEDHOF
LANGEMARCK
M.1:500

N

Early picture of the Listraum showing clearly the white stone panel embedded into the wall opposite.

were the names of all 6,313 identified soldiers buried in the cemetery, the theme of comradeship and equality in death was again emphasised as no reference to rank or religion was carved into the panels. The room also contained a cemetery register (hence the term 'list room'), the register listed names and burial plot numbers to help the visitor locate the grave of their loved one, again no mention of rank or religion was made. It was in this room that Tischler had made the first overt reference to the German student associations. Placed above the names on the wall which faced the visitor on entry to the room was a bronze plaque reading 'IHREN KAMERADEN UND KOMILITONEN DIE DEUTSCHE STUDENTENSCHAFT' roughly translated as 'YOUR COMRADES AND FELLOW STUDENTS OF THE GERMAN STUDENT ASSOCIATIONS'. On the left side as you entered the main hallway was a small room used as the guardroom. Mounted onto the exterior wall on the left was a stone plaque detailing the burial concentrations from other German cemeteries into Langemark between 1930 and 1932. The use of German stone at the entrance and the use of oak panelling in the List Room adhered to the principle of *Heimat*, the aim to create the illusion that this was German homeland albeit on foreign soil.

Left: Cemetery entrance.

Below left: The Ehrenhof and wreath looking up the Buche Allee.

be used on numerous memorials in Germany post First World War. Lersch became a staunch supporter of the Nazi party before his death in 1936.

After leaving the entrance hall, visitors entered the Ehrenhof (courtyard) and then had to turn right and make their way via a beech-lined pathway to the Ehrenfeld (The Field of Honour), or depending on the exit they chose, the main burial area the Eichenhain (Oak Grove).

The Ehrenfeld had been designed to symbolise the German front line. A stone wall was built across the width of the cemetery to separate it from the Oak Grove. Three original bunkers of the German defensive line the Wilhelmstellung remained in the Ehrenfeld, these bunkers were renovated and incorporated into Tischler's 1930/31 design plan. Fifty-one large granite blocks (reduced to forty-nine in the 1980s) were placed between the bunkers to represent the German trench line as it snaked across Flanders. In response to the requirements of the student associations, smaller concrete blocks were attached to the front of the granite blocks and carved into each were the names of the regiments and student associations who had financially supported the redevelopment of the cemetery. The naming of the area as 'The Field of Honour' had been no coincidence, the overt displaying of the names of the German student associations and organisations would forever link them to the myth of Langemark. The Ehrenfeld was sown with poppies, the symbolic

The entrances and exits to the cemetery and the Listenraum were all protected by sturdy iron gates of a lattice design and were manufactured by a Munich-based blacksmith named Karl Nowack, again the theme of the artisan had been employed. On leaving the gatehouse the visitor entered a courtyard and was immediately faced with a wall again constructed of red Weser sandstone. On this wall, directly in front of the visitor, hung a large wreath and above was the famous battle slogan of the German war poet Heinrich Lersch: 'Deutschland muss Leben, und Wenn Wir Sterben Müssen' ('Germany must live, even if we must die'). This famous quotation was to

Above: An early picture of the Eichenhain showing wooden crosses and identification plaques on the ground. The crosses in the foreground would soon be replaced in order to continue the theme of uniformity in the cemetery.

Below: 1931 Ehrenfeld plan.

wildflower that represented the blood of the German youth that had been spilt on the battlefields of Flanders.

Stepping down from the Ehrenfeld via a few gentle stone steps the visitor then entered the main burial area, the Eichenhain, the final resting place of 10,143 German soldiers. Designed as an oak grove, the Eichenhain had a mystical atmosphere, a spiritual place of German folklore. Oak trees had been

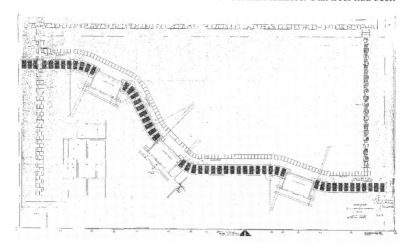

Early picture of Langemark showing the dividing wall between the Ehrenfeld and Eichenhain. Note the crosses have yet to be replaced and reorientated towards the Ehrenfeld.

planted at intervals of every 5m, and below them was a sea of 2,277 upright dark crosses (dark because of the wood preservative used) situated in a grass meadow. Tischler had decided that the burial plots in the cemetery were all to be marked by generic wooden crosses, the symbol of the cross not being used in a religious sense but purely as a grave marker so no distinction could be made based on social standing or religion. The symbol of the evanescent grave, comrades laying shoulder to shoulder as one in a forest glade, was plainly displayed in Tischler's design, as a result, the crosses were devoid of any information. The burial area of the cemetery was, in essence, an early comrades grave, a communal grave but with individual burial plots that were unidentifiable by name. The crosses had been deliberately placed to face the Field of Honour whilst the actual burials themselves were at right angles to it. In terms of design, the alignment of the crosses was more important than the marking of the burials. Each upright cross represented four graves,

in turn, each burial plot around the upright cross was marked by a small numbered flat stone so it could be easily identified via the cemetery register in the List Room. The German student associations were happy with Tischler's efforts. The design criteria had been met, Langemark had been transformed into *Heimat*, a place where the fallen lay in glory having sacrificed everything for the Fatherland. It had also cemented the bond between the German student soldiers and the student associations of the 1930s. The transformation from Langemark Nord to the Studentenfriedhof was now complete.

By the mid 1930s, the Studenten-friedhof was well on its way to notoriety. The 'Myth of Langemarck' had been enthusiastically reinforced by Hitler and his propaganda machine during the 1920s and 1930s. The story of Langemark was an unmissable propaganda opportunity and Hitler was going to exploit it to its full extent. During his trial in Munich after the failed Beer Hall Putsch of 1923 and then later from his prison cell in his

The Eichenhain showing the old entrances from the Buche Allee on the left. Note the crosses have been reorientated to face the Ehrenfeld.

writing of *Mein Kampf* he wrote of Langemark:

'And from the distance the strains of a song reached our ears, coming closer and closer, leaping from company to company, and just as death plunged a busy hand into our ranks, the song reached us too and we passed it along: Deutschland, Deutschland über alles, über alles in der Welt.'

As the 1930s progressed and Hitler and the Nazis grew stronger, many of the German youth groups started to align themselves with the far right ideas, of the NSDAP. These organisations started to make pilgrimages to Langemark, to visit the area where their fellow students had fallen. Some of the organisations who had less extreme beliefs voiced their opposition to the far right publically during their pilgrimages to Langemark. In 1934

a law was passed banning all youth organisations in Germany except for the Hitler Youth. All other German youth organisations were absorbed into its ranks and, as a result of compulsory membership announced in 1939, it had an estimated 8 million members by 1940. The doctrine of Heinrich Lersch so proudly displayed at the entrance to Langemark cemetery at the time was drilled into the members of the Hitler Youth 'Germany has to live, even if we have to die'. The Hitler Youth had become the new custodians of the Studentenfriedhof, a role they fully embraced and a role that now became one of the focal points of the organisation. By 1935 the swastika had become the sole official German flag and as a result, the pilgrimages to Langemark took on a strong NSDAP theme. Wreaths displaying the swastika became a common sight at Langemark as did large annual youth gatherings at the cemetery. Not only did the German veterans and the Hitler Youth visit Langemark during their visits, but there was also an increased presence by these groups in the 1930s at the Last Post service at The Menin Gate in Ypres. The laying of wreaths displaying swastikas at the Menin Gate was an uncomfortable image and was for some understandably unacceptable, so much so that The Last Post Association had to take away the German wreaths and ribbons at night to stop vandalism or theft. In fact in 1939, the German government made an official complaint to the Belgians after swastika-bearing wreaths had been stolen from the Menin Gate!

Bubbling just beneath the surface of some of the returning German veterans was the anger and bitterness of a generation who believed in their superiority and that they had been cheated out of their destiny. An article printed in *The Citizen* dated 23 July 1938 and written by a Mr A.W. Keith of St Andrews Scotland outlined the attitude of some of the returning German veterans. Mr Keith was a veteran of the First World War and had served with the Highland Light Infantry. In this article entitled 'From Ypres to Amiens 1938', he describes revisiting some of the areas he had served in. In the German cemetery at Langemark he had an 'enlightening' experience when he came across a German doctor and his son:

'Between the road and a field of poppies is a stretch of stagnant water. I ask the doctor if he can tell me what it is there for, as there is no apparent reason for its presence. The water is about thirty yards long by two wide and looks as though it were part of a canal. I was surprised at the result of my query. The German turned to his son, and in a voice full of unhidden hatred, he spat out the information that it was symbolic of the Belgians opening the sluices of their canals and preventing the victorious soldiers of the Fatherland reaching the Channel ports! I could not understand entirely what the father said, but I grasped sufficient to let me

German veterans laying a wreath displaying the swastika at the Menin Gate in the 1930s.

know that these poppies will again be re-dipped in blood. It is simply no use in blinding our eyes to the fact. We do not understand the Continental mind (I was told so later by a Frenchman). Anyhow, I felt I should point out to the son that as his countrymen had entered Belgium without invitation, the Belgians were quite within their rights in doing what they did to stop the invader. The father broke in, and in a torrent of language impressed, or tried to, on me that they (the Germans) would not forget and would not be caught that way again. I don't know

how tense the situation was in Downing Street on the eve of 4 August 1914, but I did know that it looked as though the poor old H.L.I. was to bear the brunt of it as usual unless I could pour oil on troubled waters! Taking the son by the arm, I turn him around and pointing to those thousands of crosses, say how futile it all was, whether for the winner or the loser. I should have saved myself the trouble. He is not an individual, but part of the fatherland, and the question of his becoming clay, at the age of 25 is of little moment if it is in the interests of Germany.'

Left: Inside the Langermak Halle.

Bottom: Modern German street sign bearing the name Langemark Street.

violent death, but one of glory, honour and martyrdom. Langemark had become a state-sponsored myth. The elevation of Langemark from a physical defeat to a spiritual victory was complete with evidence in plain view all over Germany – roads, town squares, bus stops, rail stations – many were renamed in honour of Langemark, in fact even today a few Langemarckstrasse's remain (Essen for example) and Langemarckplatz in Koblenz. Many social initiatives launched by the state had the term Langemark attached to them, the Langemarckstudium, the Langemarck Sacrifice, there was also the Book of Langemarck even youth hostels were named Langemarck. During the 1936 Berlin Olympics, the Nazis had named the main building in the Olympic Stadium Langemarck Hall. Full of reference to the Kindermord, it contained seventy-six regimental flags and a symbolic grave containing soil from the cemetery in Langemark, even an SS Division was raised from Flemish volunteers later to be named the SS-Sturmbrigade Langemarck.

It seems the propaganda machine had done its job, the myth of Langemark was an absolute gift and they used it to its full extent. The German public, looking to restore the self esteem and honour of Germany readily digested the party line on Langemark. The official story was not one of tragedy and

On the 10 May 1940, Germany invaded Belgium and in the space of eighteen days it achieved what it failed to do in the four years of the First World War, the complete occupation of Belgium. From 28 May 1940 until 4 February 1945 Belgium was occupied by German forces and was, in effect, an unwilling member of the Third Reich. The history of the Studentenfriedhof was about to enter a new phase.

4: AN INCONVENIENT TRUTH: THE 'JEWISH QUESTION'

The inauguration of Langemark German cemetery on 10th July 1932 came just under a year before the first official anti–Jewish laws were passed in Germany. In 1933 a raft of legislation was passed designed to remove Jews, Communists and 'Non-Aryans' from positions of influence in society, effectively making them third-class citizens with little or no protection from the law. In sweeping changes it became illegal for German Jews to work in the German civil service or to practise in the legal profession as judges or barristers; German patients who saw a 'non-Aryan' doctor would not be covered under the national health insurance and so excluded Jewish doctors from German society; the Nazis limited the number of Jewish students enrolled in German schools to 1.5 per cent of the total enrolment; Jews were excluded from owning farmland or engaging in agriculture and by July 1933 Jews could be stripped of their citizenship. This attempt to marginalise the Jews from German society and remove them from German history now became a problem for the Nazis with regards to their portrayal of the Kindermord. The myth of Langemark portrayed the German students as the social elite, the Nazis, of course, had taken it a step further in terms of racial profiling, and no mention had been made of the 'non-Germans' involved. The racial mix in the ranks was somewhat different to the story told to the German public and more than somewhat underplayed by the official line taken by the NSDAP. In fact a good proportion of the soldiers involved in the Kindermord were what was described then as ethnically non-German or, in more extreme cases in later years, as Untermenschen. The inconvenient truth for the NSDAP was that the ranks of the so-called student soldiers, the soldiers who they portrayed as the social elite of Germany, included a healthy proportion of (amongst others) Danes, Serbs, Poles and Jews. Not only was this an uncomfortable fact for the NSDAP but the irony was Robert Tischler in his design for the List Room had put it in plain sight for everyone to see. By walking into that room and reading the names carved into the oak panels it became apparent that there was a large portion of 'Non-Aryan' names amongst the 6,313 known burials.

Not all of this went unnoticed by the visiting German student associations. Not all German student associations were far right organisations and not all agreed with Hitler and the Nazis particularly on racial policy, the absorption of these associations into controlled groups was yet to happen, and some of these associations did not hold back in voicing their opposition to the unjust treatment of their Jewish comrades who fought and fell at Langemark. The following is a translation of an article printed in *Die Weltbüehne* in 1933 concerning a German student associations visit to Langemark:

Two hundred and fifty participants in the 16th German Student Conference took part in an excursion to Flanders. They were addressed by their leader, G. Krüger in the cemetery of Langemark. He ended with the words, 'Where we are standing today is a piece of Germany. Germany is wherever Germans gave their life and blood for their people.' The

Belgian officials were very cooperative. There were no incidents to report during the excursion. In stark contrast to the incident in November 1914, as the British machine guns and the insane commands of their own General Staff were cooperative in mowing down a few thousand German grammar school old boys and students. This piece of Germany lies directly outside the miserable brick settlement which has inherited the name of the destroyed village of Langemark.

In it is the ten thousand whose names are carved into the walls of a fenced-off niche of the ceremonial entrance gate, and whose remains rest under plain black wooden crosses, strictly aligned, so straight that no inspecting superior officer would be able to subsequently find fault with it. Two living German gentlemen call 'Heil Hitler!' but there is no one there to reply. The porter opens a heavy iron gate to the morgue. Inside is like a classroom: two benches with desks. On the wall hung wreaths instead of school caps. They are black, white and red and decorated with swastikas: 'To our fallen comrades, from C.V.', 'To our dear dead, from the German Male Voice Choir' … There is a black register containing the names, units and grave numbers of all the scholars and students, alphabetically, on one of the desks. There is another column for notes. It is empty. No praise, no censure. So these are the candidates for death who passed the patriotism test, the model students with whose conduct one rebukes the living. The Germans, and the non-Germans. The result of the examination cannot be changed: there are two Lewys, two Seelig and a Kohn. The volunteer Kurt Salomon was a doctor, but the boycott cannot reach him. He can represent his Arian colleagues here. No. 5314 is called Rosenbaum, and that does him no more harm than the following

Rosenkranz and Rosenthal. Jacobsohn (6531) didn't make it to the concentration camp or into exile. Abraham, who forced his way to the front of the dance of death, wears only his ID, not a humiliating star. Pollak, Heimann and Bär: they fell without satisfying the criteria of the race laws, 'to have taken part in at least three officially recognized battles.' Lots of Meyers: you can't tell. The name doesn't contain Jewish racial characteristics, and the Arian osteology knows no others. My schoolmate D. looked 'terribly Jewish'. He collected butterflies and was going to be a doctor, but in 1915, he changed track and became a voluntary defender of his fatherland instead. Now he is lying alongside Arians who are no longer in a position to protest against his presence. 'Volunteers first!' demanded the fatherland in 1914. 'Death to the Jews!' it demands in 1933. My friend D. obeyed both demands to the letter. Attention! 'We are standing on a piece of Germany.'

Die Weltbüehne magazine was shut down by the Nazi authorities in March 1933.

The voices of dissent against oppression and injustice were quickly drowned out by a German government determined to pursue its goal. There was however one instance when Hitler and his propaganda machine potentially had to stare the Langemark myth full in the face. That instance was Hitler's visit to Langemark German cemetery. In June 1940 during his tour of the old Western Front Hitler stopped for a brief thirty-minute visit to Langemark to honour the fallen students of the Studentenfriedhof and take advantage of a massive propaganda opportunity. Hitler was accompanied by his personal photographer Heinrich Hoffman who recorded his every step. Hoffman was fully aware that non-Germans and especially Jews were buried in the cemetery and to acknowledge that on film would have been a propaganda disaster. To negate any potential issues the visit was very carefully choreographed. Tischler's design of the Oak Grove as a communal grave in the 1930s with its theme of uniformity in death helped solve at least part of this problem for Hoffman, all of the graves were marked by generic wooden crosses so there was no chance of a Jewish grave marker being inadvertently pictured. The real problem was the List Room which displayed the names of the 6,313 named burials in the cemetery, with non–German and Jewish names in full view. This potential embarrassment had already been solved in the 1930s by amongst others the Hitler Youth. From reading quotes of visits at the time it seems the List Room had a barrier across its doorway barring entrance and hanging on its walls were wreaths bedecked in swastikas. As quoted in Chapter 3, our Scottish friend of the H.L.I Mr A.W. Keith, wrote in *The Citizen* on 23 July 1938, about his visit to Langemark where he met a German doctor and his son, in the article he describes his entrance into the cemetery, 'Entering the doorway is a porch, on the right of which is a sort of annex railed off. In the annexe are two huge Nazi wreaths with the swastika prominently displayed'. It seems that Hitler walked straight past the List Room on entering and leaving the cemetery, and so negated the possibility of any ill taken photographs that might have generated a few awkward questions. There is documented evidence that in the German military cemetery in Cambrai France, Hitler ordered that all the Jewish gravestones with the Star of David be removed and replaced by a cross with the inscription 'Unknown German Soldier'. The Nazi motto at the time was 'No Jew can have fallen for Germany'.

There is, however, no evidence to suggest this being the case in Langemark, there were no Jewish grave markers in the main part of the cemetery in the first place and secondly, Hitler never visited the List Room where the names are carved into the oak panels.

There was of course anti-Semitism in Germany as in the rest of Europe pre-First World War. Many German Jewish men fought for their country not only out of pride but in the hope they would become accepted into mainstream German

society. Lieutenant Josef Zürndorfer died when his aircraft crashed in 1915. In his will, he wrote 'As a German I went into the field to protect my beleaguered fatherland. But also as a Jew, to fight for the full equality of my fellow believers.' An estimated 100,000 German Jews answered their country's call during the First World War of which approximately 12,000 were killed, 17,000 of them were awarded the Iron Cross Second Class; and 1,000 were awarded the Iron Cross First Class; 2,000 were officers and 1,200 were military doctors and civil servants. The youngest German volunteer was a Jewish student, born in Constantinople in 1904, Josef Zippes, who was mobilised in 1917 at the age of 13 years old. He lost both legs in battle and died in 1934. After the war, in an attempt to shift the blame of defeat onto the Jews and Communists with the so called 'stab in the back', the far right described Jewish soldiers as slackers and defeatists.

The longed-for equality never did materialise.

On the 1 June 1940, Hitler revisited the First World War battlefields of Northern France and Belgium. Touring the areas in which he had served during the Great War his motorcade was destined to end up in the Ypres Salient. After visiting Ypres and the Menin Gate he was driven to the Studentenfriedhof at Langemark for a carefully planned and choreographed propaganda opportunity. Hitler's personal photographer Heinrich Hoffman plus a film crew were permanently at his side during the whole of his tour, their job was not only to document the tour but to show the German public that Hitler was in effect as good as his word, the wrongs of the First World War had been righted, the honour of Germany had been restored not by the old order but by Hitler and the Nazi Party. A visit to Langemark by the Fuhrer to pay his respects to his fallen comrades of the First World War was potentially a propaganda gold mine, the chance to reinforce the spiritual link between the students of Langemark and the Nazi movement and of course its head, Adolf Hitler himself.

At Langemark everything was in place for Hitler's arrival. As the motorcade approached the main entrance to the cemetery, the main road, the Klerkenstraat, was flanked either side with well-placed enthusiastic German soldiers in rows four or five deep, who surged forward to get a glimpse of their leader as he stepped down from his staff car. For added effect, the outer wall of the cemetery was lined with members of Hitler's personal bodyguard standing shoulder to shoulder overlooking the sea of burial crosses in the Oak Grove. Inside the cemetery were strategically placed groups of soldiers and photographers, the whole atmosphere of the visit was a strange mix of reverence, triumphalism and the celebrity of Hitler. By assessing the photographs taken by Hoffman and a short cine film taken of the visit we can put together, as best we can, the movements of Hitler during his brief visit to the Studentenfriedhof. On arrival Hitler was welcomed by General von Schwedler of the IV German Army Corps. Hitler and the General strode through the entrance hall and past the List Room. There is some evidence to suggest that the List Room had a barrier across its entrance and now contained wreaths from visiting German organisations and the Hitler Youth giving it a shrine-like appearance. On entering the courtyard (Ehrenrof) both Hitler and

Official magazine of the Volksbund Deutsche Kriegsgräberfürsorge (VDK) depicting Hitler's visit to Langemark in June 1940.

General von Schwedler turned right and walked along the beech-lined pathway, every move being captured on film by Hoffman. Ignoring the entrances to the Oak Grove (Eichenhain) they entered the elevated area known as the Honour Field (Ehrenfeld). It was here that arguably one of the most famous photographs of his visit was taken by Hoffman. In the photograph Hitler stands in front of one of the First World War German bunkers that had remained in situ in the cemetery and looks at the names on the granite blocks into which the names of the donors to the cemetery are carved. (Many a tour guide has used this photograph as a reference point so clients can literally stand in the footsteps of one of the world's most evil men, an unnerving feeling no doubt). Having looked across the Oak Grove (Eichenhain) at the field of dark wooden crosses marking the burials of his past comrades, he then leaves the Honour Field (Ehrenfeld) via the same beech-lined pathway used on entry. Hitler then exited the Studentenfriedhof via the main entrance to the adulation of the waiting German soldiers outside. He climbed into his motorcade and departed having cemented his link to the legend of Langemark into history. The whole visit lasted no more than about thirty minutes.

There were, however, some surprising omissions during Hitler's visit, for example there are no photographs of him laying a wreath at Langemark in honour of the sacrifice made by his comrades in 1914, although there are many pictures of Hitler in the Honour Field (Ehrenfeld) and of his entrance and exit of the cemetery there seem to be none of him walking amongst the graves and crosses in the Oak Grove (Eichenhain).

Hitler standing in the Ehrenfeld looking across the Eichenhain.

Photographs were taken of him looking at the crosses from a distance, for example; over the wall before he entered the cemetery and from the Honour Field (Ehrenfeld), but I can find no photographic evidence of him actually walking amongst the oak crosses in the Oak Grove (Eichenhain) itself. That would have been as they say today 'the money shot' but yet the highly experienced Hoffman and his propaganda team apparently failed to take it, just as they failed to have a photograph of Hitler in the List Room looking at the names carved into the oak panels that lined the walls. Was this a time issue? (as this was a whirlwind visit), an oversight (hard to believe given the experience of the propagandists involved) or was there another motive, a political motive, a way of dealing with a rather inconvenient truth. Whatever the reason, Hitler was never to return.

During the Second World War and the German occupation of Belgium, the Studentenfriedhoff still received visits from German organisations and many ceremonies were held, particularly on major anniversaries, Langemark Day (11 November) for example. The cemetery also seems to have had a contingent of German soldiers stationed on site, highlighting the importance of the site to Nazi mythology. A few pictures exist of Second World War German soldiers using the bunkers in the Honour Field (Ehrenfeld) as shelter having connected the entrances of all three bunkers via a trench, other pictures show German soldiers brewing coffee around the entrance to the bunkers.

Although Hitler never returned to the cemetery his treatment of the Belgian people in the Second World War was to have a far-reaching effect,

not just on the Studentenfriedhof at Langemark but all the German burial sites in Belgium. During the occupation, the responsibility for the care of the German cemeteries was transferred over to the German Army (the Wehrmacht) and the official German Grave Service. The case of Langemark was slightly different, it was privately funded and managed by the VDK as opposed to the official German Grave Service so as a result its management was taken over by members of the Hitler Youth who saw it as their moral duty to look after what had become their spiritual home. The VDK was relieved of responsibility and was in effect sidelined for the duration of the Second World War. During the period of occupation between 1940 and 1944, the Nazi government demanded that the Belgium state now paid for the upkeep of the German cemeteries in Belgium, thus rendering the Belgian/German graves agreement of 1926 null and void. The balance of power had shifted, and once again the war dead were being used as political pawns. Most of the cemetery staff were retained but were supplemented by forced labour, local Belgian people from the area where the cemeteries were situated. Refusal to do the work or desecrating the graves in the cemeteries was met with harsh punishment. From the British perspective the burial grounds of the IWGC fell into some disrepair as the staff of the IWGC had left Belgium in a hurry during 1940 and tried to make their escape via Dunkirk. Some local people did care for the British cemeteries as best they could, and to be fair to the German occupiers, there was no policy of systematic destruction of Allied war graves or monuments. Lots were damaged in the fighting of 1940 and 1944 (the Menin Gate for example) but, with a few exceptions, most were left alone by the Germans.

The occupation of Belgium was a severe and brutal experience for the population and was as bad as it was anywhere else in Europe. The Jewish communities of Belgium were rounded up and transported east for 'processing'. Many Belgian men were required to report for forced labour and were sent to Germany, some never to return. Food was scarce as the Germans implemented a policy of strict rationing, curfews were put into place and anyone caught outside during the curfew was in serious trouble. Some Belgian civilian families were ordered to billet a German soldier in their house to whom they had to give up their best bedroom and make sure was well fed. Many men and women simply disappeared, arrested under the infamous and shadowy 'Nacht and Nebel' order (Night and Fog). Issued on 7 December 1941 by Adolf Hitler the order enabled the disappearance, imprisonment and death of so-called political activists and resistance members whilst leaving the family and the population with no idea of the fate or whereabouts of the alleged offender. In many cases victims who disappeared in these clandestine actions were never heard from again. For many Belgians, this was not the first, but the second German occupation they had experienced in their lifetime, and as a result by the end of the war most Belgians hated the Germans with a passion. Eventually in early September 1944, just a few months after the D-Day landings in Normandy, Ypres and its surrounding areas were liberated by the Polish 1st Armoured Division. After four years of repression and near starvation, the Belgian people were free. The Germans had finally gone. The winter of 1944 was a notoriously harsh winter with recorded temperatures in the Ardennes on the Belgian border reaching as low as minus 28 degrees Celsius at night. After four years of German occupation, food was scarce and there was a desperate shortage of fuel. Coal was virtually impossible to get hold of, so in an effort to survive the winter the Belgian populous started to look for alternative fuels to burn, wood of course being the most obvious choice. The cemeteries of the hated, but now departed, occupier provided a perfect source of timber, row upon row of wooden crosses and oak trees now became the target for a population who were in desperate need of warmth. Sentimentality did not come into the equation; these were the cemeteries of the hated enemy and this was literally a choice between life and death. The German cemeteries provided an understandable solution to a desperate situation. In a report compiled in 1949 it was estimated that anything up to 45,000 wooden crosses plus trees from German cemeteries had been turned into firewood by the local population during the winter of 1944/45, in short some of the smaller German cemeteries had been virtually stripped clean of grave markers.

During the period of the 1950s major design changes were made at Langemark, many of which are still in evidence today. To understand the rationale of these changes we must first look at the immediate post-war period and the general situation in Belgium in relation to the First World War burial sites. The 10 November 1944 was a significant date in this process. The Belgian government chose this date as the day they took back control of the German burial grounds and prohibited the Germans from having any jurisdiction over them. Thirty years earlier the date of 10 November had also been very significant, this time to the Germans, as it was the date, they claimed the Kindermord had taken place at Langemark, resulting in the infamous 'Myth of Langemark' and all its National Socialist links. Was this date selection a conscious decision by the Belgian government? … I leave it for you to decide. The German cemeteries ended up being maintained by two Belgian associations, Nos Tombes/ Onze Graven and the Belgian Red Cross. Having surveyed the hundred or so remaining German cemeteries, the Belgian government found they could have extensive repairs (and therefore costs) to make. The survey detailed that around 80,000 wooden grave crosses placed by the Germans from the 1920s onwards were now either rotten or in poor condition, there was also the best part of 45,000 wooden crosses missing which the locals had turned into firewood in 1944/45. Many of the trees in the cemeteries had also been cut down during that period, their rough stumps now bearing new shoots in the cemeteries affected, the German cemetery in the town of Menin being one of those most badly hit. The Belgian government made a start by replacing some of the wooden crosses with cheap concrete alternatives, but the level of upkeep was, understandably, at best minimal, so the German cemeteries once again became neglected and overgrown. Ironically the Studentenfriedhof at Langemark does not seem to have been as severely affected by the locals need for firewood in 1944/45 as some of the other German cemeteries. Several pictures exist dated 1946 still showing a sea of oak crosses in the then badly overgrown Oak Grove

(Eichenhain), but how many of the crosses were rotten or in a bad state of repair cannot be judged from the photographs. By 1949 the Honour Field on the northern side of the cemetery (Ehrenfeld) was completely overgrown.

Not only was the cost of maintaining the German cemeteries an issue to the Belgian government, but public opinion was also becoming a factor, particularly in the Ypres Salient. At the end of the Second World War there were c.130 First World War German cemeteries in Flanders. As the Great War in Belgium quickly got bogged down and remained static for four years it is of no surprise that the majority of the remaining First World War cemeteries were located in the areas where the majority of the fighting had taken place, West Flanders, the Ypres Salient to be more exact. Most of the farms in the area had been family owned for generations and in terms of hectares/acres were quite small units compared to today's large cooperatives, the average size of an arable farm being

The density of the oak trees in the Eichenhain.

10 hectares at the time. Many of these farms had multiple cemeteries on their land, both Allied and German. From a Belgian landowner's point of view the siting of Allied cemeteries on your land was not a problem, after all, the fallen of those nations were responsible for liberating Belgium. The German cemeteries were more of a problem, however, as they were the burial places of the invader, the hated enemy who had twice occupied Belgium, repressed its population and reduced them to near levels of starvation. In short, the Belgian farmers wanted their land back. So, in the early 1950s, the Belgian government started to push for a new war graves agreement between themselves and Germany, with the main aim of transferring the responsibility of German war grave care back to the Germans and so releasing themselves from the associated costs. The Belgian government approached and held talks directly with the only remaining German war graves organisation the VDK. Once again, the Belgians held a strong hand in the negotiations and pursued their

Langemarck Duitsch Krijgskerkhof.
Deutscher Kriegerfriedhof.

goals with a steely and ruthless determination. The Belgians had other aims also, a reduction in the number of burial sites, so the use of the land could be returned to its rightful owners and a demand for compensation for the costs incurred when looking after the German war graves during the Second World War. To help 'focus' the minds of the German negotiators at the time the Belgians had ceased all forms of maintenance in the German cemeteries and from the start of 1952 closed them to all visitors including German delegations. The negotiations were concluded on 28 May 1954 when an agreement was reached between the two parties. The new agreement came into force retrospectively from 1 January 1954.

The new agreement stipulated that the West German government would be responsible for the maintenance and all associated costs of the German cemeteries in Belgium. The Germans also agreed to pay 18,000,000 Belgian Francs in compensation to the Belgians for the maintenance costs of the German cemeteries between 1940 to 1954. The most dramatic and far-reaching part of the agreement was the reduction of c.130 First World War German burial sites down to only four. An estimated 112,000 German bodies were to be exhumed and then then reinterred in four of the existing cemeteries selected to remain. The cemeteries chosen were Menin, Vladslo, Hooglede (although originally selected Hooglede was never actually used for this purpose and its burial rate remained much the same) and of course 'The Studentenfriedhof' Langemark Nord. All four of these cemeteries were designated to become collection cemeteries. In return the Belgian government agreed to officially expropriate the land for the four remaining cemeteries and make it available to the Germans at no charge providing it was used for war graves, thus giving the Germans the same rights afforded to the Allies for their cemeteries. Tax and logistical benefits were also offered to the VDK. The Germans were to pay for all the exhumation and transport costs for the process of concentrating the burials whilst the Belgians would supply the actual labour. Although the work was to be done by the Belgians the work was to be overseen by German officials. The German authorities were happy with the agreement as not only did it give them back control of their cemeteries, but it reduced the cost base of 128 burial sites down to four, and as the VDK was funded by donations the site reduction was an important financial factor. As in 1926 with the first Belgian/German burial agreement, the compromise found seemed to be a happy solution for both parties.

When the VDK had reformed in 1946, despite his National Socialist links, Robert Tischler was retained as its chief architect. By retaining Tischler in his role the VDK could guarantee a continuity in design with the expansion of the four selected cemeteries. Tischler duly set about the task of redesign but with always keeping the old design principles in mind. Between the years of 1955 to 1957 the VDK exhumed and relocated 111,334 German and 578 French soldiers. We will focus on arguably the most extensive redesign, that of the Studentenfriedhof, Langemark German cemetery.

The Belgian/German war graves agreement of 1954 gave the VDK total responsibility for the management of Langemark and the mid to late 1950s saw major design changes in the cemetery. The agreement of 1954 required that the burials in the 128 remaining German cemeteries were to be exhumed and relocated into four chosen concentration cemeteries of which Langemark was one. This meant that in Langemark's case the burial rate would soon rise from *c*.10,000 to *c*.44,000. Although the Belgian government had given the use of the land for the four existing cemeteries it had not agreed to any expansion of the cemeteries to accommodate the extra burials, so in Langemark an extra 34,000 bodies had to be buried in a cemetery originally designed for 10,000 burials. Clearly a major redesign was needed.

The chief architect of the Volksbund Deutsche Kriegsgräberfürsorge (VDK), Robert Tischler, set to work and the early 1950s saw the start of the redesign process. In an effort to solve the problem of the missing and rotten grave markers, all of the remaining wooden crosses were removed from the burial area of the cemetery, the Oak Grove (Eichenhain), and were replaced by 5,000 small oak blocks 8 x 4.5 x 25cm installed at ground level with the grave reference number engraved into a copper panel attached to the blocks. Tischler also installed thirty-six sets of five graduating basalt crosses in the Eichenhain. The basalt crosses were designed to facilitate a change of mood in the cemetery. The crosses were first planned to be installed in the 1940s and were designed with a militaristic theme in mind, that of the hierarchy of the army, the larger cross of the five representing the officer in charge. The VDK, for obvious reasons, rejected any idea of military symbolism post the Second World War and although the crosses were installed, they were now designed to reinforce the theme of peace

1969 cemetery plan.

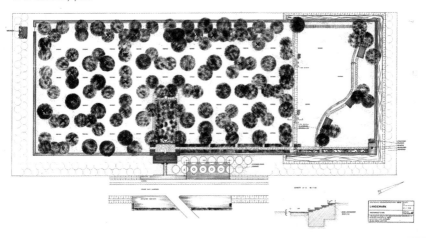

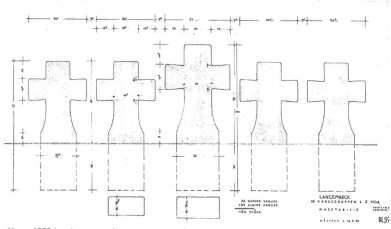

Above: 1953 basalt crosses dimensions.

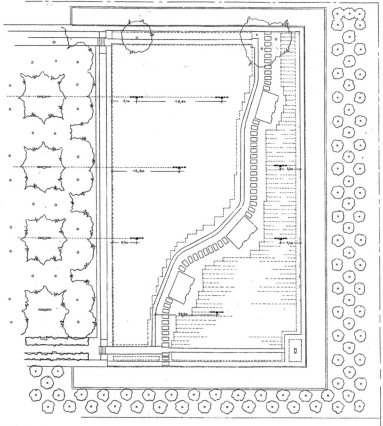

1956 plan showing the basalt crosses in the Ehrenfeld.

The Eichenhain in 1951.

and serenity in the cemetery. The oak trees around the basalt crosses were cleared so to give the impression of a forest glade. With the sea of wooden crosses now removed, the cemetery took on a much softer feel, the image of mass burial had been replaced with one of calm, peace and serenity, the now inconspicuous graves resting side by side in a communal burial area blending with the surrounding nature. At the same time some of the willow trees planted on the boundary of the cemetery were thinned to help integrate the cemetery into the surrounding landscape. The German design principles of the 1930s, nature and comradeship, were still plainly in evidence in the 1950s during this new chapter of Langemark's evolution, it should of course be of no surprise that this National Socialist feel should be carried on, as it was Tischler in the 1930s who had designed Langemark cemetery in the first place.

Between the years of 1955 and 1957 Langemark cemetery swelled dramatically in terms of burials. To accommodate the extra 34,000 bodies Tischler drastically altered the cemetery design. The Honour Field (Ehrenfeld) was now turned into a secondary burial area. This area had originally been designed to honour the names of the student associations and other organisations who had funded the cemetery in the 1930s, their names being carved into the granite blocks that linked the three bunkers on the northern side of the cemetery. Space was needed in the cemetery to cope with the increase of burials, so the Honour Field was cleared of the wild poppies and approximately 10,000 identified First World War German soldiers were reburied in the 3,100sqm of its grounds. This was almost as many burials as there were in the original part of the cemetery, the Oak Grove (Eichenhain), which was three times the size of the Honour Field at 10,000sqm. The individual grave size in the Oak Grove measured 150 x 65cm and each grave contained either single or multiple burials. The grave size was dictated by the fact that the burials at that point in history were either full or partial remains which had not yet entered a complete state of decomposition. In contrast, the burials taking place in the Honour Field (Ehrenfeld) were nearly forty years after the end of the First World War and so had completely decomposed into a skeletal condition. As the longest bone in the human body is the femur, with an average length of 48cm for an adult male, a grave size of 70 x 50cm was more than sufficient. Each set of remains was contained in a jute bag coated in bitumen and tied at the top with a zinc name plate attached. Each grave had double occupancy so to allow for the approximate 10,000 burials and were individually marked with a small oak block onto which was mounted a copper plaque bearing the first and last names of the two occupants of each grave site. 5,116 blocks measuring 8 x 4.5 x 25cm were installed in this area.

By far the biggest change to the cemetery during that period was the construction of a mass grave known as the 'Kameradengrab' or the 'Comrades Grave'. It had been decided by the VDK that all the unknown soldiers buried in the 128 German cemeteries would be exhumed and then reburied in one location only, the site selected was Langemark. Once again Tischler was determined to stick to his design principles and the naming of the mass grave as the 'Comrades Grave' reflects that. By naming it as he did, Tischler once again gently coerces the mind away from the violence and mass death associated with a mass grave, to a completely different feeling of

brotherhood and spiritualism which was evoked by the term 'Comrades Grave'. The creation of a Comrades Grave at Langemark was also to serve another purpose, the VDK wanted to create a focal point of commemoration for those German families who had lost loved ones in Belgium during the First World War but had no identified grave to visit. Robert Tischler's specified dimensions for the Comrades Grave was 12 x 20 x 1.7m, (roughly the size of a tennis court) this excluded the grassed top layer and the stone edging blocks. Built as an ossuary it contained just under 25,000 sets of human remains. After forty years of decomposition the sets of remains were purely skeletal, some sets were complete, and some sets were at best 'partial' which explains why the equivalent of a crowd in a medium sized football stadium could be buried in an area the size of a tennis court. The remains were again contained in bitumen coated jute bags and were stacked carefully into the ossuary. During the excavation of the ossuary several graves from the original burial area, the Oak Grove, had to be moved to release the space required for the construction of the Comrades Grave, these were then reinterred at the

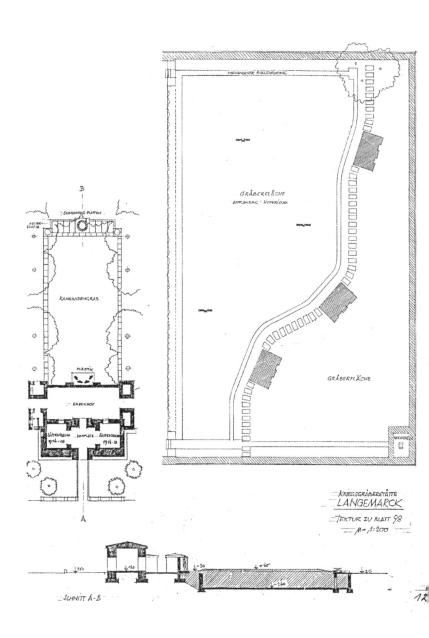

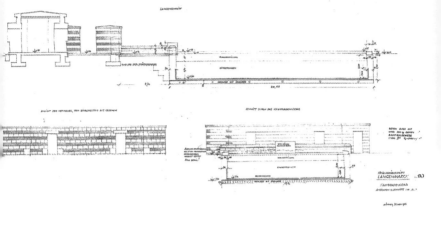

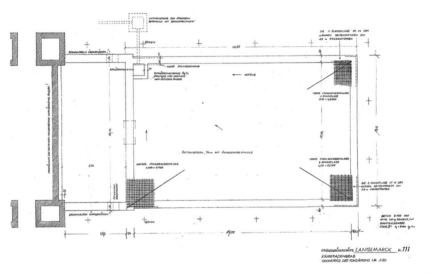

Top and opposite: 1954 Kameradengrab plan.

Above: 1955 cemetery plan.

same time as the new burials in the Honour Field on the northern side of the cemetery. The construction of the Comrades Grave also required the removal of two sets of the basalt crosses thus reducing the total in the cemetery to thirty-four groups up to that point.

The years of 1957 to 1958 saw more extensive changes to the layout of the cemetery. The first change concerned the opening of a new room on the

Right: Design model of the Kameradengrab.

Below: Early picture of the Kameradengrab. Note no statues or provincial plaques are in place.

left-hand side of the entrance hall opposite the List Room (Listenraum). The new room on the left-hand side had previously functioned as a guard room (Wärterraum) and had a stone panel embedded into the outer wall detailing the cemeteries which had been closed and their burials relocated to Langemark during the 1930s. Tischler's design required the demolition of the left side wall thus

opening up the old guard room to the same area specifications as the List Room opposite. The stone panel was removed and stored for later display. This new space was again clad in oak and carved into the oak panelling on the wall facing the gated entrance to the room was a map of Belgium detailing the sites of the 128 German cemeteries which had been closed and their burials concentrated into the four remaining cemeteries including Langemark itself. Carved into the oak panels on the left-hand wall as you entered the room were the words 'DIE HEIMAT GEDENKT IHRER IN LANGEMARCK RUHENDEN GEFALLENEN DES KRIEGES 1914–1918' (The homeland remembers the fallen of the 1914–1918 war who rest here in Langemark). This room was described on the plans at the time as the 'Weiheraum' (Sacred Room). A more subtle change was the adding of a line of text to the Heinrich Lersch quote that faced the visitor as he entered the Ehrenhof 'Courtyard of Honour.' Underneath the original line of 'Deutschland Muss Leben, und Wenn Wir Sterben Müssen' (Germany must live, even if we must die) the words 'Heinrich Lersch 1914' were added. The subtle addition of the date gave the quote a historical reference point and therefore took the ownership of the quote away from the far-right groups of the 1930s. This was a conscious attempt to break the link between Langemark cemetery and the far right politics of the 1930s and 40s.

The period of 1957 to 1958 saw the completion of the Comrades Grave. At the western end of the grave, nine stone slabs were placed, one large central slab and four smaller slabs either side. These smaller slabs displayed in bronze, the coats of arms and the names (in German) of eight Belgian provinces where the cemeteries containing the unknown burials had been located, those provinces being FLANDERN (Flanders), HENNEGAU (Hainaut), BRABANT (Brabant), ANTWERPEN (Antwerp), NAMUR (Namur), LIMBURG (Limburg), LUTTICH (Liège) and LUXEMBURG (Luxemburg). There were in fact nine Belgian provinces but in the interests of symmetry the provinces of East

and West Flanders were merged into one under the collective name of 'Flanderen'. The central stone slab was the centre piece of the design. Mounted on the top of this larger slab was a substantial bronze wreath, constructed of bronze oak leaves, the wreath remained faithful to the German design principles Tischler had applied in the 1930s. In the centre of the wreath was a biblical quote: 'ICH HABE DICH BEI DEINEM NAMEN GERUFEN. DU BIST MEIN (Jes. 43.1.)' 'I called you by your name. You are mine' (Isa. 43.1.). The stone slabs were flanked on each corner of the Comrades Grave by two large and elaborately designed iron candelabras for use on specific commemoration dates, again an echo of the 1930s and the mass Nazi rallies of the era. At the opposite end of the Comrades Grave a large bronze statue of four grieving German soldiers was placed. Designed by the German sculpture Emil Krieger the statue is said to have been based on a photograph taken in 1918 and then published in the German press. The photograph depicted a line of German soldiers standing at the graveside during the burial service of their comrades. Once all of the unknown soldiers from the 128 German cemeteries had been exhumed, transported and laid to rest in the Comrades Grave, the ossuary was sealed by a partition wall so space was left for future burials.

Work also continued at the northern end of the cemetery on the Honour Field, a further addition came in the guise of three sets of five basalt stone crosses and three new oak trees mirroring the new design of the adjacent Oak Grove. At the same time the new burial area was laid to lawn to allow easy access to graves and planted with St John's wort (Hypericum). The

large stone basalt cross (Hochkreuze) that stands in the north-east corner of the Honour Field was also put into place at the same time. Robert Tischler, the chief architect of the VDK and the main designer of Langemark died suddenly in 1959. Tischler left a design legacy that had been tainted by his connections to the far right and his close links to Hitler and the Nazis. Tishcler's design influence is still clearly evident in Langemark today. For the next decade after Tischler's death no new additions or design changes of note were implented at Langemark.

In the late 1960s and early 1970s Dr Georg Fischbacher was the head of the construction department of the VDK. He was responsible for the design changes at Langemark and was assisted by Horst Howe the representative of the VDK for all the German military cemeteries in Belgium and France. As an architect, Fischbacher was a man of his time. Germany was keen to

Above: Kameradengrab with statues and provincial plaques in place.

Below: The inspiration for Emil Krieger's statue.

Top: Ehrenfeld showing the five cross installations and early planting.

Above: The Ehrenfeld overgrown.

Left: The Ehrefeld showing the problem of grave identification due to the height of the planting. Note the new height of the boundary wall.

disassociate itself from its National Socialist past and was still in the grip of collective guilt from the Second World War, factors which would influence the design evolution of Langemark cemetery in the coming years.

The first major change that Fischbacher made was the installation of new grave markers in both the Oak Grove (Eichenhain) and the Honour Field (Ehrenfeld). This drastic change directly contradicted the German design principles of the 1930s as it removed the ideal of the comrades burial, men indistinguishable in death. The flat black granite stones were rectangular in shape and laid flat on the floor in the middle of grave groups, one stone per eight graves in the Oak Grove and one stone per sixteen graves in the Honour Field. Fischbacher was responsible for

the design, creation and installation of the new 'pillow stones'. In order to accommodate the new pillow stones and allow for their installation the groups of stone basalt crosses in the Oak Grove and the Honour Field were removed

The Hoch Kreuz.

and then replaced. In the Oak Grove the thirty-four groups of five crosses were reduced to twelve groups of three, both small crosses from either end of each group being removed. There is little documentation to explain why, however, in the light of the funding arrangements of the VDK (*see chapter on the VDK on p125*), it's not unreasonable to assume they were taken to other cemeteries to be used as a cost saving exercise. The placing of the pillow stones in Langemark solved two problems for the VDK, one practical and one ideological. The first practical problem was that the small grave markers placed at ground level in the Honour Field and the Oak Grove were constantly being obscured by the St John's wort and the grass that had been grown in their respective areas. The placing of the pillow stones at a height of 8cm (and the removal of the St John's wort and returfing in the Honour Field) meant that the grave markers were clearly displayed and easy to read.

The second problem was one of ideology. Although subtle attempts had been made to break the design link between the cemetery and the far right of the 1930s, the cemetery was still virtually of the same design as it was when Robert Tischler first designed it in the 1930s with all its National Socialist connotations. The placing of the pillow stones which now crucially displayed name, rank and date of death was one more way of dissociating the cemetery from the original design theme. Gone was the National Socialist ideal of the community grave, the theme now portrayed was one of mass death, sorrow and futility. Fischbacher was starting to make his mark. The stone wall built across the

Above left:
Recent burials.

Left: Looking from the Ehrenfeld into the Eichenhain. The dividing wall is gone but the basalt cross groups have yet to be installed.

Later photograph showing the grass slope and the basalt cross installation.

width of the cemetery to separate the Ehrenfeld from the Oak Grove was also demolished during this period.

Another subtle break with the far-right ideology of the 1930s came with the installation of a stone slab outside the main entrance to the cemetery. Carved into the Weser sandstone tablet (matching the stone at the main entrance) was the five-cross symbol of the VDK and the words: 'DEUTSCHER SOLDATENFRIEDHOF 1914–1918 LANGEMARK'.

What's in a name you ask? Potentially a lot is the answer. Historically, in an attempt to take ownership of Langemark, the Germans had always used its traditional spelling ending with a 'ck' ie Langemarck as it mirrored the German spelling. This spelling of Langemarck was in evidence all over Germany during the 1930s and 40s and so became closely related to not only the Langemark myth but also, of course, to Hitler and the far right. Hitler and the far right chose to use its original spelling in an effort to Germanise the location. When analysing the official plans of the cemetery the spelling of Langemark highlights the political nuances of the architechts and designers at the time.

For example, on the pre 1930s German plans Langemark is spelt as it is today, it then changes to Langemarck on German cemetery plans of the 1930s at the height of the National Socialist era, and then in the plans of 1970 reverts back to its correct modern spelling of Langemark. Carved into the left-hand side of the rough hewn column at the cemetery entrance is the German spelling of 'Langemarck', carved in the 1930s the intention was to carve that spelling into eternity. The placing of the new name stone in the 1970s with the correct Flemish spelling was perhaps the new German designer's nod in acknowledging a wrong which had to be righted. This small but important change removed another link to the politics of the 1930s. The placement of the stone is an indicator of the designer's desire to reinvent the cemetery, no longer called the 'STUDENTENFRIEDHOF', the cemetery started to be presented as the 'SOLDATENFRIEDHOF' or the 'Soldiers cemetery'. The name change in fact corrected history, the reality was the cemetery was never really a Studentenfriedhoff as portrayed by the far right as the student casualties were only a small ratio of the original burials in the cemetery. The massive increase in burials in the 1950s of course decreased that ratio even further. The renaming of the cemetery can also be traced on the architect's plans – the plans of the 1930s using the term Studentenfriedhof whilst those of the 1970s label the cemetery as the 'Soldatenfriedhof'. Once again another link to the far right had been being removed.

Still under the design guidance of Georg Fischbacher the years 1983/84 saw the next major design changes in Langemark. The first change concerned the Comrades Grave and came after research into the Bavarian state archive revealed the names of all missing soldiers who had served in Bavarian units in Belgium during the First World War. The Bavarian archive (unlike the Prussian archive) had survived the Allied bombing of the Second World War and so was at least partially able to name the missing Bavarian soldiers of the First World War in Flanders. As one of the aims in creating the Comrades Grave was to provide a point of commemoration for the thousands of German families who had lost a loved one in the Great War but had no grave to visit, it was agreed to position thirty-four upright basalt lava blocks around the edge of the Comrades Grave, this has since increased to thirty-eight blocks as a result of the cemetery redesigns in later years. Mounted on each side of the blocks were bronze panels, stamped into the panels were the details of 17,342 German soldiers lost in Belgium with no identified grave. The majority of the names of the missing came from the Bavarian state archive with some additions from family members of the fallen who had contacted the VDK with the details of their missing relatives. Some of those would have been already interred in Langemark, some in the remaining German cemeteries in Belgium but a good proportion were still laying in the battlefield, their remains still waiting to be recovered. The German Army at the time was divided into the armies of Prussia, Bavaria, Saxony and Württemberg, only the Bavarian First World War military records survived the destruction of the Second World War and so we will never know how many German soldiers from the other three armies were lost in Belgium during the Great War.

The second change was to demolish the wall in the courtyard (Ehrenhof) which faced the visitor on entry. The Heinrich Lersch quote of 1914 was removed from the wall and placed above the door as you entered the courtyard. Virtually unnoticeable in its new position, the quote so beloved of the Hitler Youth in the 1930s and 40s had been consigned to almost obscurity in the cemetery. The removal of the wall necessitated the moving of Emil Krieger's statue of the four grieving soldiers to the western end of the cemetery facing inwards towards

Outside the main entrance.

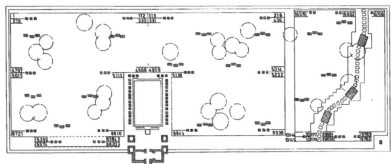

Above: 1982 cemetery plan.

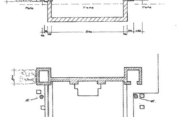

Above and left: 1983 plan showing cross section of the Comrades Grave.

Below: 1984 cemetery plan.

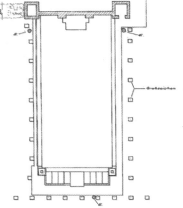

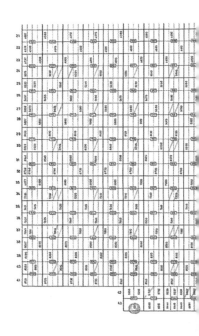

the main entrance. The silhouette of the statue was now framed by the entrance doorway and immediately drew the visitors gaze whilst inducing the feelings of tranquillity, sadness and loss. Once the statue had been relocated the eight bronze plaques displaying the shields of the provinces of Belgium and the large centre plaque of the bronze wreath were moved to the eastern end of the Comrades Grave. On entry to the cemetery the visitors' focus was taken to the plaques on the Comrades Grave and the statues on the horizon. Fischbacher also ordered that the wall separating the Honour Field from the Oak Grove be dismantled and replaced by a sloping grassed embankment with sets of gentle steps leading down to the Oak Grove, it was at this point that the three sets of basalt crosses in the Honour Field were removed completely.

The visitor could now view the cemetery from one corner to another with an uninterrupted view of the lines and lines of pillow stones. The view across the Oak Grove emphasised the sheer scale of the losses and reinforced the underlying message of the futility of war. The old design ideals of the 1930s had been laid to rest by Fischbacher, the cemetery no longer focussed on the glory of the soldier's death and the honour of dying for the Fatherland. The new design themes were of peace, sadness and senseless death. This was the cemetery of the defeated, an invader of two world wars who in their quest for atonement had publicly and sincerely embraced these new themes. Georg Fischbacher had put his design stamp on Langemark. By making relatively simple changes Fischbacher changed the whole mood, character and underlying message of the cemetery.

The transformation from Studentenfriedhof to Soldatenfriedhof was now complete.

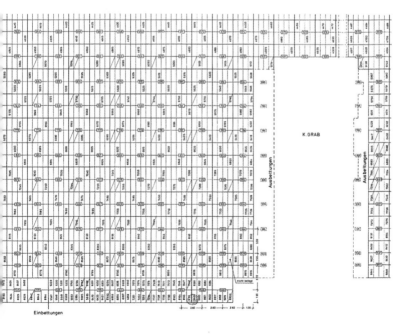

Early picture of the installation of the pillow stones.

7: LANGEMARK TODAY

Today's Langemark and recent burials

The more recent design changes to the cemetery have been for practical rather than ideological reasons. The opening of the In Flanders Fields Museum in 1998, the 80th anniversary of the end of the First World War plus various television and book releases all helped to promote a new awareness of the Great War amongst the general public by the late 1990s. Coupled with the opening of the Memorial Museum Passchendaele in 2004 the battlefields of Flanders saw a steady increase in visitor numbers from countries across the world, and as a result Langemark German cemetery started to see an increase in footfall. In 2002 Langemark German cemetery was made an official listed monument by the Belgian Government meaning it could apply for funding from the Belgian authorities. In anticipation of increased visitor numbers, a car park and visitor centre were constructed in 2006. The visitor centre/entrance tunnel, was designed by the architects Govaert & Vanhoutte from Brugge. The long black tunnel consists of several TV screens showing a brief history of the cemetery plus some information boards to educate visitors on the history of the cemetery before they enter its grounds.

The last major renovation of Langemark to date took place in 2015. The €274,000 project was deemed necessary because of the anticipated increase of visitor numbers during the centenary commemorations of the First World War. As Langemark is classed as a protected monument the Flemish government contributed 50 per cent of the renovation costs. The foresight was well placed as during the centenary commemorations an estimated 1.1 million visitors paid their respects at Langemark. The renovation work was extensive and again succeeded in altering the overall design of the cemetery. The companies responsible for the work were the Zonnebeke-based architect Andy Malengier BVBA, with the building work being completed by Monument Vandekerckhove NV. As part of the work, the existing pavements and terraces were renewed, the floor of the inner courtyard re-laid as was the pathway around the Comrades Grave. In addition, new pavements were laid, stairs were renovated and drains constructed as the Comrades Grave had become liable to flood. Lawns were redeveloped, hedges cleared and a suitable access pavement for the disabled created. The pillow stones in both burial areas of the cemetery were taken up and then re-laid on concrete bases to stop them sinking into the ground and to give them all uniformity in height. The pillow stones which had been pushed up by the roots from the oak trees were moved to the next adjacent stone, all the pillow stones were then cleaned and the names and details re-whitened.

The most significant change related to the Comrades Grave and Emil Krieger's mourning soldiers statue. It was decided to move the statue back to its original place at the eastern end of the Comrades Grave in line with Emil Krieger's original intention. The wall which the statue backed on to, and which was demolished under Georg Fischbacher's design of the 1980s, had to be rebuilt. By moving the statue and rebuilding the wall, the modern-day

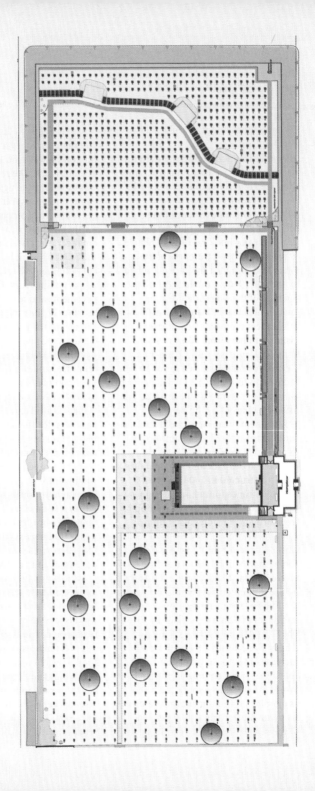

2015
cemetery
plan.

architects had inadvertently restored part of the cemetery to the plan of Robert Tischler and the far right of the 1930s, however, the Heinrich Lersch quote remained as it was and out of immediate view. In preparation for the rebuilding of the wall, the path at the far end of the Comrades Grave had to be extended to create a wider terrace area so several of the original burials dating from the 1930s were exhumed and then relocated elsewhere in the cemetery. The creation of the terrace made space for the plaques of the eight Belgian provinces and the large central plaque of the bronze wreath which were to be moved from the eastern end of the Comrades Grave to its western end. The widening of the terrace gave extra room for groups of visitors to stand and read the plaques and view the statue of the Mourning Soldiers at the far end of the grave as originally planned by Emil Krieger. In the interest of continuity two extra basalt lava steles were added to the existing steles on either side of the Comrades Grave, with no brass name plaques the two steles serve no other purpose than to make the job neat and tidy and provide the option to add names of future identifications.

Today's Langemark is a blend of differing design traits which were influenced by the politics and financial restraints of the time. Much of the old 1930s design remains intact but the subtle changes made by later designers have managed to give the cemetery an altogether different feel. The one thing that has remained consistent is the use of the cemetery as a political tool. The visits of the far-right German student associations of the 1930s have been replaced by visits of the modern youth who are keen to learn from the mistakes of history, the ideals of the 1930s and 40s have been replaced

by the modern ideals of peace and reconciliation with many symbols around the cemetery reflecting these sound principles. There is also a balance to be struck between modern-day design and the local tourist industry. Whilst the German authorities are keen for the cemetery to be known as the Soldatenfriedhof, a name which has no political connotations, the local tourist industry promotes the cemetery as the Studentenfriedhof a name which has strong links to the far right of the 1930s and 40s.

There are 44,000 German soldiers laying in Langemark, every one of them once a son, a brother or a father, however, the burials at Langemark are not forgotten, it is very common to see poppy wreaths, poppy crosses and other memorials placed on the pillow stones or at the front of the mass grave. Although a few will be placed by visiting relatives of the fallen or by dignitaries at major commemorations the majority are placed by visiting school groups of all nationalities who come here to witness the futility of war. Some of the pupils may well have relatives buried in Langemark, I have witnessed on more than one occasion a pupil reading a poem to her classmates at the Comrades Grave in honour of a relative, moving to tears her fellow pupils and onlookers alike.

In general, the level of upkeep in Langemark is as good as it could be when you consider the low level of state funding the VDK receives. Relying heavily on charitable donations the VDK must spread its resources around the world as best it can, in 2019 it had a budget of €52m, of which only one third was government funded with the balance being made up by charitable donations. This is in stark contrast to the Commonwealth War Graves

Commission who are completely government funded and have a budget of €72m in 2019/20 and employs over 900 gardeners worldwide. There are no full-time gardeners at Langemark, instead a local Belgian gardening company is contracted to cut the grass and remove the leaves as and when needed, arranged by the caretaker who lives close by. Once every two years or so, volunteers from the German armed forces will donate two weeks of their time to provide general maintenance in the cemetery and clean and re-whiten the names on the pillow stones. When working in the cemetery these guys quite often become the centre of attention to the visiting guests who like to ask them questions about the cemetery and compliment them on their work. Credit for funding must also be given to the Government of Flanders. By making all four of the German cemeteries in Flanders protected monuments in 2002 they became one of the few governments around the world outside of Germany to partially fund the upkeep of those cemeteries, Langemark of course included.

Recent burials and details

By the end of the First World War an estimated 80,000 German bodies were unaccounted for in Belgium with a large proportion of those lost in the Ypres Salient. The destructive power of the artillery resulted in the obliteration of grave sites, shrapnel and high explosive shells ripped men to pieces and many bodies simply sank into the mud of Flanders leaving no visible trace. Over one hundred years has passed since the end of the First World War, and yet the battlefields of Flanders still regularly relinquishes its grip on the often-fragmented remains of the soldiers who lay hidden beneath its surface. The post war searches for graves and bodies were scaled down in the 1920s and since that period there have been no large-scale searches for missing remains in the Ypres Salient. The battlefields of Flanders have returned to their rightful use, that of agriculture and urban development. The majority of remains found today are as a result of third-party activity, for example, road building, construction projects, farming or even people digging their gardens. On an average year maybe twenty to thirty sets of human remains are recovered but if there is major building or archaeological works in progress the recoveries might run into the hundreds. The recoveries will include soldiers of all nationalities of which a percentage will be German remains. The process of body recoveries in Belgium is strictly controlled by law and anyone found contravening the law can be severely punished in the courts. The discovery of suspected human remains must be reported to the local police and the remains should be left untouched and in situ. The police will then try to ascertain that they are First World War remains and not that of a missing person for example. Once this has been established a local archaeological team will take over the process. The archaeologists will painstakingly record every detail of the remains to aid with identification and then remove the remains whilst carefully looking for any artifacts and for the possibility of any further remains on the site. On completion of their investigations the archaeologists will then release the remains back to the Belgian police who, in turn, hand the remains over to the Belgian War Graves Commission

The Kameradengrab and statues before the restoration of 2015.

who then release the remains to their relevant national authorities, in the case of the Germans the Umbettungsdienst (reburial department) of the Volksbund Deutsche Kriegsgräberfürsorge (VDK). In terms of possible identification of the remains the Germans have a slight advantage over the British remains. The British ID tags mass produced in the First World War were made of a vulcanised asbestos fibre which famously rots away in wet ground making them illegible in most cases when they are recovered today, the German Army, however, issued ID tags made of a zinc alloy which, although not perfect, is more likely to stand up to the rigours of the wet ground conditions in Flanders, therefore slightly increasing the chance that the remains can be identified at an earlier stage in the process. On receipt of the remains the Exhumation Department of the VDK (Umbettungsdienst)

will carefully log every aspect of the remains in an individual document relevant to that set of remains only. They record the ID tag details if recovered, the remaining clothing and other belongings/equipment, height of the individual, details of the skeletal remains and also a detailed dental record is taken, all in the hope of future identification if needed. Once completed the remains are then released for burial at a future date.

There have been several burials in Langemark since the completion of the Comrades Grave in the 1950s. Once the grave was completed and sealed a small crypt was left with the expectancy of future body recoveries and burials. The crypt entrance is concealed under the Flandern slab at the far end of the Comrades Grave. There are no more burials in the Oak Grove or the Field of Honour, all burials take place in here. The

German policy is to have large burials in terms of numbers as it is more cost effective, the remains are placed into small coffins measuring 68 x 35cm and are then passed down into the crypt during the commemoration service. Time is a great healer and the burials at Langemark are now well attended not only by the German authorities, but by local dignitaries, town mayors, local remembrance organisations and members of the general public. There is also a great deal of media interest which quite often turns the commemorations into a high-profile event.

One such high-profile event took place on 12 October 2019 when the remains of eighty-four German soldiers of the First World War, only three of which were identified, were interred in the crypt at Langemark, this being the largest interment in the Comrades Grave in recent years. The majority of the remains (seventy-three sets)

were recovered during archaeological work at the former German position known as Hill 80 on the outskirts of the village of Wijtschate (Heuvelland). The archaeology project was financed partly by crowdfunding and partly by the VDK who donated €25,000 to the project. With the help of a multinational team of volunteers, the archaeologists recovered German, British, French and South African remains. The scale of the reburials and the high level of media interest ensured that the service was a high-profile event attended by many invited dignities, remembrance organisations and members of the general public. In preparation for the service a marquee was erected as a seating area for the dignitaries at the end of the Comrades Grave and flowers were placed at intervals on the pillow stones. The remains of the fallen had been placed in small black coffins and were carefully laid on the

The Kameradengrab today.

surface of the Comrades Grave awaiting their reburial. Each black coffin was decorated with a ribbon of the German national colours and a single white rose (the symbol of peace and innocence) was placed on the top of each casket. Outside the entrance of the cemetery European, Belgian and German flags were raised to symbolise the themes of unity and peace, themes which are so important in today's modern Europe. At the conclusion of the service, lines of German soldiers carefully passed each individual casket down into the crypt where they were finally laid to rest after being lost for over one hundred years in the battlefields of Flanders.

The centenary commemorations of the First World War proved to be a major factor in healing the old wounds left by two world wars. On several occasions, heads of the once warring factions attended remembrance services together, standing side by side they remembered the war dead of all countries whilst driving home the message that this should never be allowed to happen again. For me, Langemark cemetery as it is today reflects that message perfectly. It is a place not only of serenity but one of sorrow and reflection. Fate deals us cards that we have no control over, had I or you been born in Germany during that period we could very easily be laying in Langemark cemetery today. If there is one lesson we can take away from Langemark German cemetery it is this, the motto of the VDK 'Arbeit für den Frieden' or 'work for peace'.

Modern-day burial in the crypt, 2019.

The Langemark German cemetery of 2021 is a combination of differing design styles that evolved from the changing political map of Western Europe in the twentieth century. The political climate at the time was to heavily influence the designers of the cemetery. From the original Great War designs, the Kindermord, the influence of the Nazis in the 1930s and 40s to the post Second World War designs and the effort to de-politicise the cemetery, all these elements are still in evidence in the cemetery today. Sometimes the different elements exist harmoniously side by side virtually unnoticed, whilst some seem to clash head-on, reflecting the chaotic political landscape of its era. Ironically this modern era of peace and reconciliation and its design changes has resulted in the two most obvious and contentious contradictions of the intended underlying modern theme of the cemetery. The first being the re-siting of Emil Krieger's statues back to their intended position at the head of the Kameradengrab, mourning the loss of their comrades who lay beneath their feet. Because of the different design changes they now stand with the Heinrich Lersch quote, so beloved of the Nazis, in full view above their heads. Whilst it can be argued that the addition of the date of 1914 to the quote puts it into its correct historical context there can be no arguing that this is a clash of intended design and its intended symbolism.

The second design contradiction is much more obvious and has resulted from the increased visitor numbers to the cemetery and all of the touristic benefits attached to it. The German authorities, as the title of this book suggests, had spent a lot of time and effort post Second World War in changing the underlying design theme of the cemetery, steering it away from its National Socialist messages and reinventing it as a place of tranquility, peace and reconciliation. As a result of this reinvention the official road signage guiding people to the cemetery uses the words 'Deutscher Soldatenfriedhof' or the 'German Soldiers cemetery'. Unfortunately in their quest to encourage tourism (and understandably so), the local authorities have overlooked this fact and have placed their own touristic route signage beneath the official sign, the new sign boldly declaring 'Studentenfriedhof' or 'Student Cemetery'. Of course this sign has been placed with the events of the Kindermord in mind but what has been overlooked are the strong links to Hitler and the Nazi party that this name evokes, something I would have thought would be 'uncomfortable' for a formally occupied country. Clearly this signage has been placed with the best intentions in mind, but now having learnt of the story behind the name I hope you the reader, much as I do, will have a wry smile when you come across it on entering the car park.

PART 2:
SELF-GUIDED TOUR

INTRODUCTION

Lies, Damned Lies and Statistics

One of the problems facing writers and researchers of the First World War is the accuracy of published statistics. In the years after the war, published statistics varied greatly and depended on when they were written and who had published them.

Quoted casualty figures for example can vary significantly, after the Great War some were inflated for political gain in an effort to discredit the High Command of the time, some were inaccurate as a result of lack of or poorly recorded documentation and some were inaccurate due to a lack of understanding of the terminology used. A good example of this is the well used and often misinterpreted term of 'casualty'. When quoted correctly the term accounts for the combined figures of killed, wounded, missing and prisoners of war, it is not, as some have published, a figure of those killed. This misunderstanding has led over the years to wildly inaccurate figures of men thought to have been killed – the Battle of Passchendaele is a point in question. So, as with everything in life treat Great War statistics with an element of distrust and caution.

The same ethos of course applies to the statistics linked to Langemark German cemetery. Virtually from day one, the figures for the amounts of original burials have varied from official sources, this is mainly due to lack of documentation and the restrictions faced by the Germans in terms of managing their cemeteries as a result of two world wars. In addition to this, graves have been moved from one part of the cemetery to another and of course every year there are new burials in the crypt of the Kameradengrab which are not recorded overtly anywhere in the cemetery, so hand on heart I cannot say the statistics printed here are 100 per cent accurate to the man, but they are as close as they possibly can be. The Volksbund Deutsche Kriegsgräberfürsorge (VDK) themselves seem quite happy to admit that because of the lack of documentation they treat Langemark as a 'monument' and that the figures are not up to date and the bodies are not necessarily buried where the grave markers say they are.

The only important statistic is this, Langemark German cemetery contains the burials of *c*.44,000 human beings of all ages and from all walks of life, each one was once a father, brother or son with their own hopes and dreams but whose lives were cut brutally short by the carnage of the Ypres Salient.

Right: The Entrance tunnel.

Opposite: The chemical ceapons attack signpost.

Below: Plan of the tour route.

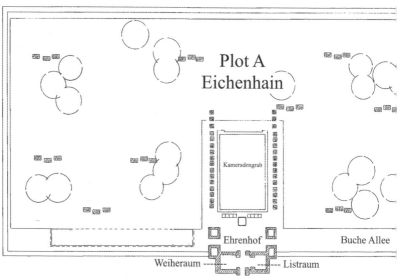

On leaving the car park walk towards the cemetery via the tunnel structure on the gravel pathway. Opened on the 26 August 2006, the tunnel serves the purpose as an information centre prior to your entry into the main part of the cemetery. The three double TV screens and information boards give a brief history of the German War Graves Commission (VDK), the battles of Ypres including the gas attacks of 1915 and the history of Langemark cemetery itself. Once you have watched and read the presentations please exit the tunnel at the far end into an open terrace area.

As you look towards the northern end of the cemetery you will see some recently installed information boards outlining the history of the cemetery. Having read the boards walk to the pathway past the signpost marking the sites of gas attacks around the world since 1915 and look at the corner of the cemetery where you will see the first two examples of the original cemetery design.

1. The Hochkreuz or High Cross. Installed in late 1957/early 1958 the 1.52m basalt cross stands on the north-eastern corner of the cemetery. Shaped as a traditional Teutonic cross it boldly announces the existence of the cemetery to passers-by.

2. The Wassergraben or Moat. The ditch immediately below the Hochkreuz which surrounds the northern wall and going around to the

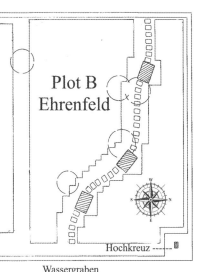

Wassergraben

eastern wall dates from the original design of the 1930s. The moat reflects the original German design principles, 'The cemetery grounds would be separated from its surroundings by a moat or a low wall to emphasise the sacrosanct nature of its grounds'. In Langemark's case the Wassergraben also came to represent the flooding of the Yser plain by the Belgians in 1914 which prevented the outflanking of the Allied forces by the German Army and the fall of the channel ports. Please refer to Chapter 3, p37, and the quote from the article printed in *The Citizen* dated July 23rd, 1938 and written by a Mr A.W. Keith of St Andrews Scotland with reference to this.

3. Now continue along the willow-lined avenue towards the main entrance to the cemetery. As you walk through the tunnel of willows look to your right for your first glimpse across the cemetery grounds. The cemetery is enclosed by a 1m thick stone wall with an earth and grass top.

4. As you reach the main entrance to your left stands a small Weser sandstone tablet. Installed in the early 1970s the upright tablet confirms

the transition of the cemetery from Studentenfriedhof to Soldatenfriedhof. The correct spelling of Langemark confirms the rejection of the cemetery's historical links to the far right of the 1930s. Also displayed is the five-cross symbol of the VDK.

5. You are now standing in front of the main entrance to the cemetery. In accordance with the original German design principles, the entrance hall is constructed out of Weser sandstone originating from Lower

Above: Welcome to Langemark. **(5)**

Opposite: Avenue of Willows. **(3)**

Left: A dry Wassergraben with the Hoch Kreuz above. **(1)**

Above: The Main Entrance. **(5)**   *Right:* The Weser stone entrance pillars. **(6)**

Saxony. Either side of the doorway, carved into the rough-hewn columns, are the words 'Langemarck' (in the German spelling) and the dates 1914–1918 in Roman numerals. Dating from the early 1930s and measuring approximately 13 x 5m, the imposing entrance hall is part of Robert Tischler's original design.

6. Main entrance. Walk up the steps and go through the narrow doorway and enter the Vorraum (Vestibule). Pre 1955 this area was known as the Ehrenhalle (Honour Hall) but the name changes on the post 1955 plans to the more functional Vorraum, or Vorplatz, possibly another example of the designers trying to shake off the National Socialist past of the cemetery. Having entered the Vorraum you will see two rooms, one to the left – the Weiheraum and one to the right – the Listenraum. Both rooms, as well as the entrance, are protected by heavy wrought iron lattice gates and screens manufactured by a Munich-based blacksmith named Karl Nowack in the early 1930s.

7. Before entering the rooms look up to the ceiling to view the mosaic of five crosses with the central cross being silver in colour. This is the second reference so far to a five-cross symbol, the first being outside on the Soldatenfriedhof stone slab. The five cross symbol is the logo used by the VDK. Over the years the use of the five-cross symbol has become controversial as it represents the five wounds of Christ during the crucifixion and does not account for the other religious denominations who fought for the German Army. There are many more references to the five crosses in the cemetery.

8. Please now enter the left-hand room, the Weiheraum.

The mosaic ceiling in the vestibule. (7)

2 THE WEIHERAUM / SACRED ROOM

In its present form, the Weiheraum or Sacred Room dates from the 1957/58 renovations to the cemetery. Previous to those dates, the room was sealed off with a small part of it being used as a guardroom and a storeroom. Embedded into its outer stone wall was a stone plaque which detailed the surrounding German cemeteries which were bought into Langemark pre-1932. Those cemeteries were closed, and their previous occupants reburied in Plot A in Langemark. On two different plans, both dated 1955, the Weiheraum is referred to as the Listenraum 1914–1918 and the Ehrenraum 1939/1945. The second name raises the possibility that the room was to be used to record Second World War German casualties in Belgium, but this was never realised. In 1957/1958 the outer wall of the Weiheraum was demolished to allow access to the room. Matching wrought iron gates and trellis were added so the Weiheraum blended in perfectly with its surroundings. Manufactured by Manfried Bergmeister, the iron work mirrors exactly the rest of the iron work in the Vorraum which was constructed over twenty years previous to this.

1. As you stand in the approximately 15sqm Weiheraum the first thing you will notice is that the whole room is clad in oak, the oak being a national symbol of Germany; representing strength and endurance, this symbolism plays a big role in the design of Langemark. The back wall depicts a map of Belgium and its surrounding neighbours. Primarily the map shows the position of the German cemeteries pre 1957 before they were exhumed and reinterred in Langemark. The map also shows the position of the four cemeteries selected in the 1950s to become collecting cemeteries, Menin, Langemark, Vladslo and Hooglede. The concentration of cemeteries in the Ypres area highlights the Belgian landowners' demands for the return of their land post the Second World War. In the bottom left-hand corner is a passage of text in German, roughly translated as 'This map illustrates the cancelled and final German military cemeteries of 1914/1918 in Belgium'. It then goes on to provide an explanation for the symbols on the map: 'Explanation of signs': 'Abandoned cemeteries whose dead was transferred to the final facilities' and 'German/French community cemeteries'.

Above: The Heimat quote. **(2)**

Below: Map of Belgium in the Weiheraum. **(1)**

2. Carved into the left-hand oak wall in the Weiheraum are the words 'DIE HEIMAT GEDENKT IHRER IN LANGEMARCK RUHENDEN GEFALLENEN DES KRIEGES 1914–1918' (The homeland remembers the fallen of the 1914–1918 war who rest here in Langemarck).

3. There is some evidence to suggest that as late as the 1990s this room contained a set of bound books recording the names of all known burials in the cemetery. The books would have been kept in the table which now stands up against the left-hand wall hence the sometimes naming of the room as the 'Listenraum'. The books no longer seem to be in existence, the internet having made them obsolete, although I have contacted the VDK about this issue. There is, however, a visitors' book which sits on top of the table allowing the visitors to record their comments on the cemetery.

4. On the right-hand side of the room, mounted in a metal frame, is the original stone plaque which was mounted on the room's outer wall before that wall was demolished in 1957. Not only does the plaque detail the cemeteries absorbed by Langemark in the early 1930s by name and reference number, but it also gives us a first indicator of the initial burial rate in the cemetery when it was reopened in 1932: 6,253 bekante (known) and 3,780 unbekante (unknown) making a total of 10,033 original burials in plot A.

Now leave the Weiheraum and cross the Ehrenhalle/Vorraum and enter the room opposite, the Ehrenraum.

Above: The stone tablet which used to be embedded into the outside wall of this room. (4)

Right: Early picture of the Listraum showing clearly the white stone panel embedded into the wall opposite.

Also known as the Ehrenraum (Room of Honour), the Listenraum (List Room) displays the names of the original identified burials which are interred in the original part of the cemetery (Plot A the Oak Grove). In contrast to the Weiheraum, the Listenraum dates from 1932 and is part of Robert Tischler's original plan for the cemetery. The pre-ordained German design principles stipulated the building of a Listenraum or Ehrenraum in order to record the names of the fallen and Tischler adhered closely to those early principles in his original design for Langemark. The early German design principles had also stated that the physical graves in the burial area of the cemetery were only to be marked by reference numbers in order to promote equality and camaraderie in death, so the graves in the cemetery displayed no names. The construction of the Listenraum fulfilled the requirement of being able to honour the fallen as individuals. These names are now duplicated in Plot A (Oak Grove) on the black granite pillow stones which mark the graves and were installed in the 1970s.

1. The approximately 16sqm room is totally clad in oak panels into which are carved the names of the identified burials in the original part of the cemetery. There are 782 blocks of eight names each and one block containing one name which totals 6,257 names on the walls. This is four more than quoted on the stone plaque in the Weiheraum and is as a result of later body recoveries.

The names in the Listraum. **(1)**

Names of many nationalities and religions. (2)

2. There are at least thirty German Jewish soldiers officially commemorated amongst the names here in the Listenraum, the VDK are still searching archives in an attempt to identify all German Jewish soldiers so this figure will more than likely rise. You will also notice many Eastern European names, mainly Polish. The boundaries of Europe were very different in 1914 and modern-day Poland was divided between Germany, Austria Hungary and Russia. Many Polish people lived and worked in Germany and so it is logical that they would find themselves in the German Army. If you refer to chapter 4 and the quote with reference to the German student association visit to the cemetery, you will find the same names as quoted here on the walls in the very room which you are standing, a good example is Dr Kurt Salomon.

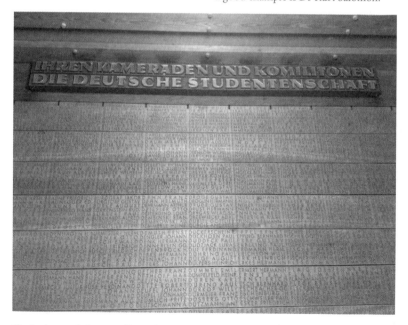

The Studentenschaft quote. (3)

ASSOCIATIONS'. The installation of the plaque was a design requirement of the German student association in the 1930s and is the first overt attempt to link themselves with the perceived glory of the 'Kindermord'.

4. The oak panels are in beautiful condition, smooth to the touch and the names are displayed alphabetically by surname.

Once you have taken your time here please leave the room, turn right and walk through the open doorway into the 'Ehrenhof' or the 'Courtyard of Honour'.

3. Placed above the names on the wall which faces the visitor on entry to the room is a bronze plaque reading 'IHREN KAMERADEN UND KOMILITONEN DIE DEUTSCHE STUDENTENSCHAFT' roughly translated as 'YOUR COMRADES AND FELLOW STUDENTS OF THE GERMAN STUDENT

THE EHRENHOF / COURTYARD OF HONOUR

The purpose of the Ehrenhof was twofold, first of all to provide a link from the Ehrenhalle to the main part of the cemetery and also to provide a partly sheltered area for wreath laying and acts of commemoration. As you enter the Ehrenhof you are faced with a wall constructed out of Weser sandstone. This is not the original wall from 1932. The original wall had a stone protruding in able for a large wreath to be hung. Above the wreath was the infamous Heinrich Lersch quote so beloved by the Hitler Youth. The original wall was demolished during the cemetery re design of 1983/1984 and then rebuilt during the last cemetery re design of 2015. The floor of the Ehrenhof was also relaid in 2015.

Opposite top: The Buche Alle today. (4)

Opposite bottom: The Heinrich Lersch quote. (3)

Below: The Ehrenhof. (1)

1. Still facing the wall if you look to your right you will look northwards up the beech-lined straight pathway towards the 'Ehrenfeld' or 'Field of Honour'.

2. If you look left, there is now another entrance to the original burial area of the cemetery known as the Eichenhain or Oak Grove. As late as 1969 this entrance to the cemetery was not in existence as the original design of the cemetery guided the visitor on a set route, that route being via the beech-lined pathway to your right.

3. Now turn around and face the main entrance hall of the cemetery which you have just exited and look above the door you have just walked through. Above the doorway is the infamous Heinrich Lersch quote 'Deutschland Muss Leben Und Wenn Wir Sterben Mussen' ('Germany has to live, even if we have to die').

The Buche Allee in the 1930s. (4)

This quote became the battle cry of the Hitler Youth and was used many times by the NSDAP at major events. In the 1930s the quote was in prime position above the wreath as you entered the Ehrenhof, however, because of its strong links to the Nazis the line 'Heinrich Lersch 1914' was added during the cemetery redesign of 1957/1958. The subtle addition of the date gave the quote a historical reference point and therefore took the ownership of the quote away from the far-right groups of the 1930s. This was a conscious attempt to break the link between Langemark cemetery and the far-right politics of the 1930s and 40s. When the wall was demolished during

the works of 1983/1984 the quote was relocated virtually out of sight where it remains today above the doorway. It is interesting to note it was not reinstated by the VDK to its original position when the wall was rebuilt in 2015. Although of historical significance it is still linked strongly to the far-right groups of the 1930s and 1940s and so is best left in its current position where it can cause no offence or become the centre of attention of modern-day far-right groups.

4. Now turn around to face the wall again and turn right to walk up the long beech-lined pathway known as the 'Buche Allee' or the 'Beech Avenue'.

You are now entering the cemetery via the pre-determined route planned by the cemetery designer Robert Tischler in 1932. The 70m long beech-lined pathway runs from the entrance gate up to the Hochkreuz (High Cross) in the corner of the Ehrenfeld. The pathway deliberately takes the visitor straight to the Ehrenfeld so to view the Eichenhain (Oak Grove) from a slightly elevated position and of course pay homage to the names of the German student associations whose names are carved into the concrete and granite blocks linking the three German bunkers.

1. As you enter the Buche Allee immediately to your right is an information board placed by the VDK (German War Graves Commission) detailing a brief history of the cemetery and burial statistics. The board reads: 'This military cemetery for war dead of the First World War was laid out by the Volksbund back in the 1930s. Even back then, the construction of this site was funded by grants from Germany, just as today the Volksbund is reliant on the donations of its members and friends in order to maintain this special commemorative site. Young people from throughout Europe help on international youth camps, where they maintain the site and build bridges of understanding. In the 22-day battle of the Yser and Ypres, the 4th Army fought on the German side. For the most part, it was made up of poorly trained volunteers: students, school pupils and apprentices. The front got bogged down here on 11 November 1914 until the end of the war in 1918. There were countless losses on both sides. In Germany,

the site soon became known as the 'student cemetery'. After the war, the official Belgian burial service transferred the German war dead from the Langemark region and reburied them on land on the northern exit out of the town, where the cemetery was laid out. At the time, the war cemetery was home to some 10,143 war dead, including 6,313 victims identifiable by name. Between 1956 and 1958, the Belgian burial service closed countless cemeteries and transferred more than 30,000 other German war dead to Langemark. Today, 44,304 victims lie here. After 1970, the Volksbund renovated the grave signs (slabs) of the individual graves. In 1984, the Volksbund redesigned the communal grave containing the more than 24,000 formerly unknown soldiers. In addition, they attached plaques to the wall around the cemetery, bearing the names of the 12,000 dead resting in peace here and whose names had been determined over the past sixty years. The dead of this cemetery admonish to peace.'

Erected in 2004, the statistics on the information board are now incorrect as there have been at least a hundred more burials in the cemetery since its installation.

2. As you walk up the $c.55m$ pathway from the gate to the steps at the entrance to the Ehrenfeld, you are following the exact same route that Adolf Hitler took on his well-documented visit to the cemetery on 1 June 1940. Accompanied by General von Schwedler, Hitler is pictured strolling up this pathway towards the Ehrenfeld.

Left: Hitler in the Buche Allee 1940. (2)

Below left: Buche Allee and Hoch Kreuz. (3)

Below right: Buche Allee today. (3)

3. Walking up the pathway you will see that the beech hedge on the left-hand side is without any breaks from start to finish. This has not always been the case as originally there were three evenly spaced entrances of 60cm wide into the Eichenhain cut through the hedge. Each entrance was marked by two Weser sandstone blocks, each measuring 50 x 60 x 40cm. These blocks still exist but are on the other side of the hedge and so out of your line of sight. Once you enter the Eichenhain they are in plain view.

4. At the end of the pathway, you are faced with two choices, either turn immediately left and walk into the Eichenhain or continue up the steps into the Ehrenfeld. In the interest of historical correctness please walk up the steps and enter the Ehrenfeld.

The original height of the boundary wall of the Ehrenfeld.

EHRENFELD / HONOUR FIELD

Like many areas of the cemetery the Ehrenfeld has been known over the years by several names. Originally called the Mohnfeld or Poppy Field this part of the cemetery contained no graves until the concentration of burials in the mid 1950s. Up to that point its purpose was purely aesthetic as it was designed to symbolise the front line and display the names of the student associations and regiments who had funded the cemetery in the late 1920s and early 1930s. Confusingly it is also marked on some 1950s plans as the Ehrenraum or Honour Room. Today it is known by the somewhat less romantic term of Deel B or Plot B. The Ehrenfeld was an elevated part of the cemetery accessed by 3 gentle stone steps through a stone wall that ran across the width of the cemetery which had been built to separate the Ehrenfeld from the Eichenhain. The outer wall of the Ehrenfeld which bordered onto the

Wassergraben was built at ground level but the wall's height was added to in the mid 1950s when it became a burial ground, evidence of the original wall's height can plainly be seen on its outer wall as you walk up the willow-lined pathway opposite the Ehrenfeld as you enter or exit the cemetery.

The renovations to the wall resulted in two of the fifty-one donor stones (which are situated between the bunkers) being removed and so reducing their number to forty-nine. The stone wall that ran across the width of the cemetery was demolished in the early 1980s and replaced with the grass embankment you see today. During the concentration of burials in the mid 1950s the Ehrenfeld had three groups of five graduating basalt stone crosses installed within its area, these were removed completely from the Ehrenfeld by the late 1980s.

Right: The dividing wall between the Ehrenfeld and the Eichenhain.

Below: The dividing wall gone. As it looks today.

The role of the Ehrenfeld changed dramatically during the concentration of graves into Langemark during 1955/56 when over 9,000 sets of remains from surrounding cemeteries were relocated into this area. At approximately 3,000sqm in area the Ehrenfeld holds roughly the same number of burials as the Eichenhain but is roughly one third of the size. Buried in the Ehrenfeld are 9,573 identified (bekante) German soldiers and 69 unknown (unbekante) German soldiers totalling 9,642 burials, all buried in an area equating to roughly one half of a Premier League football pitch.

1. Staying on the pathway walk towards the line of stone blocks which connect the three German bunkers. The blocks are from the original design plans dated 1931 and symbolise the front line as it winds its way across the Flanders battlefields. Originally there were fifty-one blocks, but this was reduced to forty-nine in the late 1950s. The forty-nine name blocks or donor stones each measure approximately 160 x 80 x 80cm and comprise of two parts, the main body being constructed of concrete whilst the attached name blocks, 60 x 84 x 35cm, are granite. The granite name blocks are attached to the main concrete blocks with bronze fixings. Carved into the front of each granite block are the names of regiments and other organisations who helped finance the creation and upkeep of the cemetery, many of these organisations were student associations of the 1930s some of which are still in existence today. Twenty donor stones are dedicated by regiments and twenty-seven are dedicated by student associations whilst two at the western end of the cemetery are blank. The inclusion of the regiments and associations on the

Top: Ehrenfeld minus the basalt crosses.

Above: Student associations still place flowers to commemorate their forefathers.

donor stones does not necessarily mean that these organisations and regiments fought in this area. Such was the appeal of the legend of the Kindermord that units wished to link themselves to the myth right up until the 1960s when the last new donor names were added to the blocks.

2. Now take the path that runs in front of the blocks and stand in front of the middle of the three large bunkers. You are standing on the spot where Adolf Hitler stood whilst reading the names on the donor stones during his visit to the cemetery on 1 June 1940.

The photograph taken at the time by Heinrich Hoffman and another by an unnamed German soldier is arguably the most famous of his visit to Langemark. Built in 1916/1917 the three bunkers are part of what was the German third line of defence in the Ypres Salient known as the Wilhelm Stellung line. The original bunkers were heavily damaged during the Third Battle of Ypres in 1917 and so were refaced and restored prior to the inauguration of the cemetery in 1932. The restoration work is detailed on plans from the VDK dated 1930. The exterior dimensions of the bunkers are 3.4m high (including underground) x 5.55m wide with an earth layer of approx. 40cm deep on top of the bunker. If you wish to see what condition the original bunkers would have been in after the war, turn left out of the car park when you leave the cemetery and then take your next left on to the Beekstraat. A couple of hundred metres or so up the road on the right-hand side stands a white obelisk, the memorial to the 34th Division. Behind the memorial is an unrestored German bunker from the same period.

3. Once you have looked at the bunkers and donor stones take some time to walk around the Ehrenfeld. Its alternative name was the Poppy Field or Mohnfeld as it was completely planted with red Flanders poppies from the 1930s to the mid-1950s. Just as the bunkers and the donor stones represented the old German front line, the poppies symbolised no-man's-land and the German blood spilt in Flanders. During the concentration of graves in 1955/56, space was needed in the cemetery to accommodate the extra burials, so the poppy field was ploughed through to make room for the extra graves.

Hitler at the bunkers, taken by an unnamed German soldier, June 1940. (2)

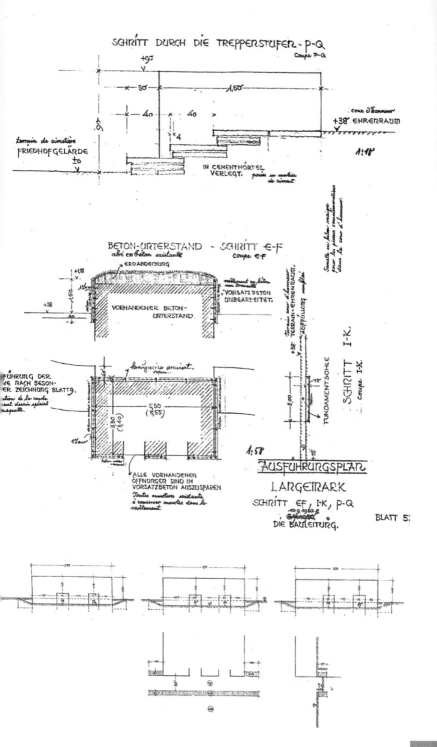

SCHNITT DURCH DIE TREPPENSTUFEN - P-Q
Coupe P-Q

+95

30 | 1,50

coux d'honneur
+38 EHRENRAUM

40 | 40

terrain de cimetière
FRIEDHOFGELÄNDE
±0

1:18

IN CEMENTMÖRTEL
VERLEGT. posées en mortier
de ciment

BETON-UNTERSTAND - SCHNITT E-F
abri en béton existante
Coupe E-F

ERDABDECKUNG

+18

VORSATZBETON
UNBEARBEITET.

+38

VORHANDENER BETON-
UNTERSTAND.

40

FÜHRUNG DER
VE NACH BESON-
ER ZEICHNUNG BLATT9.

betonneise armiert.

5,50
(5,55)

3,30
(3,40)

15cm

ALLE VORHANDENEN
ÖFFNUNGEN SIND IM
VORSATZBETON AUSZUSPAREN
Toutes ouvertures existantes
à conserver ouvertes dans le
revêtement

FUNDAMENTSOHLE

AUFFÜLLUNG

+38 TERRAIN = EHRENRAUM

SCHNITT I-K.
Coupe I-K.

1:50

AUSFÜHRUNGSPLAN
LANGEMARK
SCHNITT EF, I-K, P-Q
DIE BAULEITUNG.

BLATT 5:

The Mohnfeld. The Poppy Field. (3)

4. The existing grave markers or 'pillow stones' you see today were installed during the period of 1970/73 and replaced the small oak and copper markers originally placed in the mid 1950s. The small oak and copper grave markers quickly became overgrown and difficult to read so the larger and more pronounced pillow stones were a solution to this problem. The 609 pillow stones are of Belgian granite sourced from the Ardennes region and measure 52 x 52 x 8cm and sit in the middle of eight individual grave plots. Each grave has 'double occupancy' hence the sixteen recorded names (on average) on each pillow stone.

5. Each individual grave plot measures only 70 x 50cm and contains on average two sets of remains. The grave size is substantially smaller than those in the Eichenhain as by the mid 1950s the remains were skeletal due to nearly forty years of decomposition.

Each grave contains the remains of German soldiers whose bodies were exhumed from the surrounding German cemeteries during the concentration of burials during the mid 1950s. However, there are some burials in Plot B which were exhumed from Plot A (the Eichenhain) as the ground where they lay was needed for the construction of the Comrades Grave in the Eichenhain in the mid 1950s. As a result, these names are recorded on the oak panel walls in the Listenraum as they were original burials in the cemetery, the names on stone 16290 are a good example of this. The rest of the mid 1950 burials in Plot B are not recorded in the Listenraum.

6. Each pillow stone displays the following information:

Plot letter (Deel B) and grave reference numbers

Casualties Forename and Surname
Rank/Function or recruitment type
Date of death

7. You will notice that just before the date of death is a small cross, in this instance the cross does not represent a religious symbol but instead highlights that the date shown is the date of death. All names have the cross displayed by their date of death with the exception of German Jewish soldiers. In the 1970s the VDK in conjunction with the Jewish Council

decided that German Jewish soldiers should be recognised separately. It was decided to identify the German Jewish graves by removing the small cross next to the date of death and replace it with three letters GEF which stands for Gefallen or Fell. This negated any misconception that the small cross was a religious symbol and therefore could incorrectly mark other denominations. Currently there are thirty-two known German Jewish soldiers buried in Plot B, however, the VDK is still checking its records so the figure may well rise in the future.

8. In line with the general German design policy for cemeteries in the First World War and the importance of the symbolism of the oak tree in German mythology there are ten oak trees in this plot, four dating from the late 1950s and six from the 1970s.

9. Now walk to the top of the stone steps that lead down to the Eichenhain and look across the original burial area, instantly you will understand why it is call the Eichenhain or the Oak Grove. Now walk down the steps.

Above: Pillow stone in the Ehrenfeld highlighting the use of the three letters GEF in order to identify a German Jewish soldier. (7)

Right: Looking from the Eherenfeld to the Eichenhain, the Oak Grove. (9)

THE EICHENHAIN / THE OAK GROVE

You are now standing in the original burial area of the cemetery known as the Eichenhain (Oak Grove) or more simply Plot A. The approximate 10,000sqm area was heavily influenced by the German design principles outlined during the First World War and, as a result, the cemetery designer Robert Tischler originally planted 376 oak trees in this area, some of which remain today. The original oak crosses and their replacement grave markers were again replaced in the 1970s by the 1,110 granite pillow stones you see today. The VDK quote 10,143 original burials in Plot A in the 1930s but because of the renovations of the cemetery particularly in the 1950s when approximately 126 bodies were moved from Plot A to Plot B and a further 240 bodies were reburied in the Comrades Grave on its completion,

plus any extra burials, it is very difficult to put a precise figure on the number of burials today. The important fact, however, is that *c.*10,000 human beings are laying in an area of roughly two Premier League football pitches.

1. The deliberate use of the oak and its symbolism and the results of later design changes is still plain to see in this part of the cemetery. There are now eighty-one oak trees planted in this area of the cemetery, sixty-five from older stock and sixteen saplings planted in

2015. Through the course of time many of the original 376 oak trees have been removed mainly as a result of redesigns of the cemetery. In 2004 there were seventy-nine trees dating back to 1932 with a trunk circumference of 60–80cm plus. Some but not all are still evident in the cemetery today.

2. Twelve groups of three graduating basalt stone crosses are strategically placed around the Oak Grove. Originally placed in the early 1950s the cross groups then totalled 36 groups of five crosses (then reduced to 34 groups due to the construction of the Comrades Grave in 1956/57). At the same time, the cemetery was cleared of the remaining original grave markers (wooden crosses) and the oak trees were thinned out. The removal of the upright grave markers and the clearing of the oak trees from around the basalt crosses changed the atmosphere of the cemetery completely and underlined the design principle of a forest glade or Oak Grove. The groups of five basalt crosses were removed in the early 1970s to aid in the installation of the flat black granite grave markers (pillow stones) and then reinstated, but with the twelve groups of three crosses you see today. The original basalt cross groups were originally designed in the 1940s with a theme in mind, the five crosses represented the hierarchy of the armed forces the larger central one being the officer in charge, however, by the time the crosses were installed in the mid 1950s the VDK had rejected any idea of militarism and so the crosses were intended purely as a representation of the five-cross symbol of the VDK and also as a design feature.

The Eichenhain. (1)

Above: Cross groupings in the Eichenhain. (**2**)   *Below:* Crosses and pillow stone in Plot A. (**3**)

3. The existing grave markers or 'pillow stones' were installed in 1971 and replaced the small oak and copper markers placed in the mid 1950s which in turn had replaced the original 2,277 upright wooden crosses dating from the 1930s. The small oak and copper grave markers quickly became overgrown and difficult to read so the larger and more pronounced pillow stones were a solution to this problem. The 1,110 pillow stones are Belgian granite sourced from the Ardennes region and measure 34 x 50 x 8cm and sit in the middle of eight individual grave plots. Some grave plots contain a single set of remains whilst others contain multiple sets of remains, there is also a percentage of empty grave plots in this part of the cemetery. The long list of changes in the cemetery, the destruction and loss of some of the original grave

markers, the concentration of graves into the cemetery and poorly recorded or lost records means that the names on the pillow stones do not necessarily correspond to the bodies buried beneath them – they are buried in the cemetery somewhere, but in some cases, not where their names are recorded.

A/1489-1492

HERMANN MARSCHALL MUSKETIER · 14.1.1915
PAUL REMUS KANONIER · 1.12.1914
GEORG OEFELEIN MUSKETIER · 14.1.1915
WERNER HEESE KRIEGSFREIWILLIGER · 14.1.1915

FÜNF UNBEKANNTE DEUTSCHE SOLDATEN
KURT STENSCH KRIEGSFREIWILLIGER GEF. 10.11.1914
JOHANN FUHSY UNTEROFFIZIER · 11.11.1914
FRITZ KAUFFMANN KRIEGSFREIWILLIGER · 8.11.1914

A/1707-1710

Above: Pillow stone in Plot A The Eichenhain showing the German Jewish soldier Kurt Stensch. (4)

Left: Kurt Stensch duplicated in the Listraum. (5)

4. Each individual grave plot measures 150 x 65cm. The grave size is larger than those situated in the Ehrenfeld as these were original burials dating from the First World War onwards. The full or partial sets of remains were in a relatively early state of decomposition and so required a larger burial plot.

5. The pillow stones record the names of the *c*.6,313 identified burials in this part of the cemetery. The majority of these names are duplicated on the oak panelled walls of the Listenraum, these were the original pre 1932 burials which had been interred in unnamed graves, the names at the time being displayed in the Listenraum. The numbers of unidentified soldiers are also recorded on the pillow stones as 'unbekante' or unknown. There are *c*.3,830 unidentified soldiers buried here in Plot A.

6. Each pillow stone displays the following information:

Plot letter (Deel A) and grave reference numbers
Casualties Forename and Surname
Rank/Function or recruitment type
Date of death

7. As you walk around the cemetery reading the pillow stones you will

see many names have the word 'Kriegsfreiwilliger' (war volunteer) after their names and the date of death of mid-October to mid November 1914, these are the members of the so called 'student regiments' who were killed during the First Battle of Ypres in what was to become known as the 'Kindermord'.

8. As in the Ehrenfeld the German Jewish soldiers are identified by the three letters GEF (Gefallen) engraved into the pillow stone just before the date of death. Currently there are thirty-one known German Jewish soldiers buried in Plot A, however, the VDK is still checking its records so the figure may well rise in the future.

9. As you walk from the steps of the Ehrenfeld through the Eichenhain look to the left at the beech hedgerow of the Buche Allee and you will see the three sets of two Weser stone blocks which marked the three entrances through the beech hedge into the Eichenhain. These entrances no longer exist.

10. Walk through the cemetery heading south past the Comrades Grave on the left (east) side and head towards the south-eastern part of the cemetery. Start looking at the reference numbers on the pillow stones and locate stone number 4831 and the grave of Unteroffizier Rudolf Meier. Killed at the age of nineteen, Rudolf Meier came from the small German town of Eberbach in Baden and has the dubious honour of being the only man officially recorded in Langemark three times, once in the Listenraum, once on his official pillow stone and on his surviving original grave marker. The original grave marker is the only one of its type in Langemark and was probably paid for by his family and

Opposite: Original blocks marking the old entrances into the Eichenhain from the Buche Allee. **(9)**

Below: The original grave stone and pillow stone of Rudolf Meier. **(10)**

transported here with his remains in the early 1930s. In the bottom right-hand corner is the name of the local stone mason who produced the headstone, Timmerman Yper, the company still exists today and is situated close to the Menin Gate in Ypres.

11. Now walk back to the area surrounded by the upright stone tablets otherwise known as the 'Kameradengrab' or Comrades Grave.

The German/Belgium war graves agreement of 1954 stipulated that the remaining 128 German cemeteries in Belgium were to be exhumed and their burials relocated to four chosen concentration cemeteries of which Langemark was one. It was also decided that the unknown burials from the 128 cemeteries (c.25,000) would all be relocated to Langemark. In order to accommodate these extra burials an approximate 344sqm area in the Eichenhain (Plot A) was cleared of existing graves with 126 named burials being relocated to the Ehrenfeld (Plot B) and 240 unidentified burials stored in the Weiheraum until they could be re buried in the Kameradengrab on its completion. In 1955 work commenced on the construction of the Kameradengrab, and once the ground was cleared, an

ossuary measuring 22m long x 11m wide x 1.7m deep was constructed using concrete and reinforcing wire mesh. On completion in 1959 it was filled with the skeletal remains of nearly 25,000 human beings and then sealed. A 75cm top layer of soil was then added to the surface of the grave so it could be landscaped. At the same time the ossuary was sealed, a partition wall was constructed across the width of the remaining chamber to create a crypt of 1.5m long x 11m wide x 2m deep to accommodate any future burials in the cemetery. The Kameradengrab at Langemark was also to serve as a focal point of commemoration for those German families who had lost loved ones in Belgium during the First World War but had no identified grave to visit, as the largest (in terms of occupancy) official German mass grave for unknown burials.

1. Now stand at the western end of the Kameradengrab in front of the plaques. Look across the grass rectangle towards the statues. In the area directly in front of you, an area smaller than a full-sized tennis court, lay the remains of nearly 25,000 human beings, the equivalent of a medium-sized football stadium.

2. Directly in front of you lay nine stone slabs, the eight smaller slabs display in bronze the coats of arms and the names (in German) of the eight provinces of Belgium, FLANDERN (Flanders), HENNEGAU (Hainaut), BRABANT (Brabant), ANTWERPEN (Antwerp), NAMUR (Namur), LIMBURG (Limburg), LUTTICH (Liège) and LUXEMBURG (Luxemburg). The burials in the Kameradengrab originated from cemeteries located in all eight of the Belgian provinces. The central stone slab is the centre piece of the design. The substantial bronze oak leaf wreath remains faithful to the original German design principles of the 1930s. In the centre of the wreath is a biblical quote: 'ICH HABE DICH BEI DEINEM NAMEN GERUFEN. DU BIST MEIN (Jes. 43.1.)' 'I have called you by name. You are mine'.

The Kameradengrab. (**1**)

Left: The provincial plaques.(**2**)

Below: The bronze oak leaf wreath. (**3**)

Opposite: The entrance to the crypt. (**4**)

3. Beneath the bronze oak wreath are the words 'AUF DIESEM FRIEDHOF RUHEN 44,061 DEUTSCHE SOLDATEN DES KRIEGES 1914/18' '44,061 GERMAN SOLDIERS FROM THE 1914/18 WAR REST IN THIS CEMETERY. Placed in the late 1950s the figure of 44,041 is now inaccurate as a result of burials made since its installation.

4. Situated beneath the stone slab which displays the 'FLANDERN' coat of arms is a small paved manhole cover. This is the entrance to the crypt where the modern-day body recoveries are laid to rest. Sometimes the manhole cover is in view as the Flandern slab is not always immediately replaced after burial services. The crypt is never open to the public, it is only opened during burial services during which small coffins containing the remains are handed down into the crypt which is then resealed on completion of the ceremony.

5. At the far end of the Kameradengrab stand the statues of the 'Mourning or Grieving Soldiers' designed by Munich based sculptor Emil Krieger in 1956. In recent years the statues were moved to the rear of the cemetery but were again relocated in the cemetery renovations of 2015 back to their original position looking over the Kameradengrab as was originally intended by their designer. The bronze statue is said to have been based on a photograph taken in 1918 at Bouillonville in France of members of the Rheinischen Infanterieregimentes 258 (RIR 258) as they stood at the edge of a grave

Emil Kriegers statues. **(5)**

burying the remains of their comrades. Two days after the picture was taken one of their number was killed in action and as a result the picture was widely published in the German press of the time. The bronze statues stand 2.2m at their tallest point and are said to have been commisioned by special request of the cemetery designer Robert Tischler. Placed at a time when the cemetery design was evolving away from its previous National Socialist connections, the four sombre figures stand with heads bowed in a final tribute to the fallen who lay at their feet. You will notice that there are no stand out details on the statues, their form has been deliberately pared back to the bare minimum to reject the themes of militarism and glory in death; the statues reflect the modern-day atmosphere of the cemetery perfectly. Note the Heinrich Lersch quote is in full view over the heads of the statues in an unintended contradiction of symbolism.

6. Surrounding the Kameradengrab are thirty-eight basalt stone blocks, thirty-six placed in 1984 and a further two were added during the renovations of 2015. Each block measures 100 x 125 x 40cm, mounted on each side of thirty-six of the thirty-eight blocks are bronze panels listing in alphabetical order the names of 17,342 First World War German soldiers known to be missing in Belgium and who have no identified grave. The majority of the names on the bronze panels were sourced from the Bavarian State Archive whose First World War military records had survived the destruction of the Second World War. Unfortunatly the Prussian, Saxon and Wurttemberg First World War casualty records were almost totally destroyed by Allied bombing in the Second World War and so virtually no documentation exists of the majority of the Germans missing in Belgium during that period. This makes it nigh on impossible to accurately assess German casualty statistics. However, the

The name blocks surrounding the Kameradengrab. (**6**)

names recorded on the bronze panels are not exclusively Bavarian as over the course of time family members of the fallen from other areas of Germany have contacted the VDK to inform them of the details of their missing relations which were then recorded on the panels.

7. As the names on the bronze panels are of German soldiers who are missing with no identified grave in Belgium, it then stands to reason that they are not neccesarily buried in the Kameradengrab. Although their names are listed on the bronze panels that surround it, many will be buried in separate German and Allied cemeteries and of course many still lay undiscovered in Flanders fields over one hundred years after their death. A great example of this is the Prussian flying ace Werner Voss killed on 23 October 1917 and whose name is recorded on panel 63. Although it is widely told that Voss is interred in the Kameradengrab it is highly unlikely as

his field grave was destroyed in 1917 and his body was never officially recovered. He of course is listed on the panels as he is a notable name and is known to be missing in the Frezenberg area. The best way to describe the blocks is as an 'incomplete Menin Gate for the German Army', the stone blocks are in effect separate to the Kameradengrab.

8. There will of course be a percentage of non-German nationals buried in the Kameradengrab. The burials in the Kameradengrab are those of unknown soldiers of sometimes scant remains, therefore it is entirely possible that some may be soldiers from the British and Commonwealth forces, French and Belgium armies as well as Belgian civilians; we will never know for sure how many. There are three women (nurses) recorded as being interred in the Kameradengrab plus at least one Austro – Hungarian, one Italian POW and several Russian POWs (*see Part 3 for more details*).

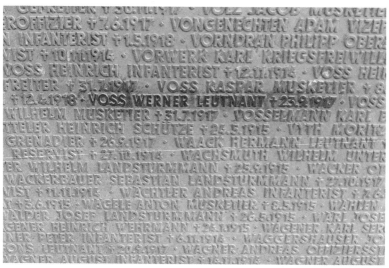

German flying ace Werner Voss commemorated on the bronze panels. **(7)**

9. Now walk to the furthest right-hand corner of the Kameradengrab nearest to and facing the statues of the 'Mourning Soldiers'. Mounted on the end of the basalt name block facing the oak tree is a small brass plaque, placed in 2004, commemorating two British soldiers whom are known to be buried in the Kameradengrab: Private Leonard Harry Lockley and Private Albert Carlill.

Private Albert Carlill died at the age of 19 on 4 November 1918 just seven days before the armistice on 11 November 1918. The son of William and Charlotte Carlill of Brough, Yorkshire, Albert died as a POW and was originally buried in a communal grave in the German section of Leuven (Louvain) town/communal cemetery amongst forty-five unidentified German soldiers. In 1956 the German graves were exhumed from Leuven Communal Cemetery in preparation for them to be moved into one of the four selected concentration cemeteries. During the exhumation process it was

discovered that the grave markers did not correspond to the bodies buried below them in the communal grave and so it proved impossible to identify Private Carlill's remains individually. Consequently the forty-six exhumed sets of remains were placed randomly in unmarked coffins and transferred to Langemark for reburial in the Kameradengrab. Up to this point the then IWGC believed Carlill's body to have been lost and so his name had been recorded on the Loos Memorial to the Missing in the 1930s. As a result of his reinterment in the Kameradengrab the VDK informed the then IWGC of the location of Private Carlill's remains in 1956 and committed to add Carlill (and Lockley's) names to the official cemetery register on completion of the works. The assistant secretary of the IWGC at that time thought it inappropriate that Private Carlill had no monument bearing his name at the place he was buried (the name blocks around the Kameradengrab were not

Opposite: The two British soldiers known to be interred in the Kameradengrab. (9)

Right: Flowers placed by the family of Leonard Lockley. (9)

installed until 1984), so it was arranged in 1956 that a 'Kipling Memorial' would be placed in Cement House cemetery close to Langemark to commemorate him and to give his family a place to grieve away from a German cemetery. No further actions were taken until after the installation of the name blocks around the Kameradengrab in 1984. In accordance with their commitment made to the then IWGC in 1956, the VDK had included the names of Carlill and Lockley on the bronze name panels surrounding the Kameradengrab. Although spelt incorrectly on the panels (Carhil on panel 10 and Lookley on panel 38) the names grabbed the attention of two local researchers Michel Vansuyt and Michel Van den Bogaert who then reported their existence to the now CWGC. So in 2004, with the agreement of the VDK, the CWGC placed the bronze plaque you see today in honour of both British soldiers. Private Carlill's Kipling Memorial was removed from Cement House cemetery and his overlooked name which still remained on the Loos Memorial to the Missing was also removed in accordance with CWGC policy in 2004.

Private Carlill has the dubious honour of being named on three memorials at the same time one of which was German: Loos, Cement House and the Kameradengrab.

Private Leonard Harry Lockley died on 30 October 1918 again very close to the end of the war. The son of Mrs E Lockley of Southsea, Portsmouth, Leonard died of wounds whilst in German hands and was buried amongst German graves in Jemappes Communal Cemetery in 1918 after which his grave was lost. After the war the IWGC arranged for a special memorial to be placed in his honour bearing his name and details and reading 'Known to be buried in this cemetery'. This headstone remained in situ in Jemappes until he was 'rediscovered' in Langemark in 2004. The headstone was then removed as he is now commemorated officially on the brass plaque placed in 2004 that you see today.

10. There are sixty-three German Jewish Soldiers identified on the name blocks surrounding the Kameradengrab, this figure will no doubt increase over the course of time as the VDK continue to update their records.

In the centenary years of 2014 to 2018 the municipality of Langemark-Poelkapelle have invested heavily in the region and have added many different monuments of differing types to the area. A few are situated just outside the official confines of the cemetery and so deserve an explanation because of the time, effort and good intentions invested in their creation.

1. The Poppy Cenotaph

In September 2016, a striking new World War 1 monument was created at the Grote Markt, in front of the In Flanders Fields Museum in Ypres, Belgium and was relocated to the German war cemetery at Langemark Poelkapelle. Standing 7m tall and weighing 12 tonnes, the metal monument features the evocative image of a single Flanders poppy surrounded by a field of 2,016 steel poppies, all handcrafted by blacksmiths and farriers worldwide. Hundreds of blacksmiths and farriers from around the world came together in Ypres and created the monument during the week-long event. Designed by Terence Clark the monument was funded by generous donations and sponsorship from companies and private individuals worldwide. Up to 2,016 poppies have been forged from steel and are arranged in rigid formation around the base of the monument, there is one white poppy to remember the victims of shellshock and whom were sometimes called cowards, these men are now rightly recognised

as Victims of War. The field of steel poppies is bordered by twenty-six railing panels. Thirteen master blacksmiths were invited from around the world to design the thirteen larger, of the twenty-five railing panels. A design competition for the remaining twelve smaller railing panels was opened to the international community of blacksmiths and designers. The twenty-five panels made at Ypres have been joined by a twenty-sixth panel, designed by Alan Dawson and made prior to the event as an example to help sponsors/donors to visualise how such a panel might be interpreted. Robert and Carol Smith travelled across England, Wales, France, Belgium, Italy and Germany forging poppies with children at schools, clubs,

Right: The Poppy Cenotaph. (1)

Opposite: The single white poppy. (1)

Left: The poppy wreath. (**1**)

Below: The gas attack audio station. (**2**)

museums and at various shows. This wonderful opportunity has enabled many children to be part of the Ypres 2016 project. The children's poppies forged at these numerous sessions have been assembled into three wreaths, one of which was laid at the Menin Gate during the Last Post Ceremony on 5 September; the other two are placed at the entrance to the Poppy Cenotaph. The completed wreaths were constructed by Robert Smith, Luc Vandecasteele, Manicx Carlieri and Rik Verschoot.

For more information, please visit https://www.yprespeacemonument.com

2. Gas attack multilingual listening post

In the corner of the car park before you walk on the gravel pathway towards the entrance tunnel stands a listening post.

This excellent innovation is one of a few placed in the area which when activated tells the story of the 1915 German chlorine gas attacks that took place in this area at 5.00pm on 22 April 1915 and so heralded the start of the Second Battle of Ypres. The use of gas was to change the war completely and ushered in a new era of mass, indiscriminate, industrialised killing. Available in four languages, the story is told by modern-day actors using quotes sourced from actual accounts of the time. If the listening post is out of use you may find below the transcript of the recording written by a German soldier of the time, Willi Siebert, who was part of the German units responsible for releasing the gas on that fateful day in 1915.

'Finally, we decided to release the gas. The weatherman was right. It was a beautiful

day; the sun was shining. Where there was grass, it was blazing green. We should have been going on a picnic, not doing what we were going to do. …

We sent the [German] infantry back and opened the [gas] valves with the strings. About supper time, the gas started toward the French; everything was stone quiet. We all wondered what was going to happen.

As this great cloud of green, grey gas was forming in front of us, we suddenly heard the French yelling. In less than a minute they started with the most rifle and machine gun fire that I had ever heard. Every field artillery gun, every machine gun, every rifle that the French had, must have been firing. I had never heard such a noise.

The hail of bullets going over our heads was unbelievable, but it was not stopping the gas. The wind kept moving the gas towards the French lines. We heard the cows bawling, and the horses screaming. The French kept on shooting.

They couldn't possibly see what they were shooting at. In about fifteen minutes the gun fire started to quit. After a half hour, only occasional shots. Then everything was quiet again. In a while it had cleared, and we walked past the empty gas bottles.

What we saw was total death. Nothing was alive.

All of the animals had come out of their holes to die. Dead rabbits, moles, and rats and mice were everywhere. The smell of the gas was still in the air. It hung on the few bushes which were left.

When we got to the French lines the trenches were empty but in a half mile the bodies of French soldiers were everywhere. It was unbelievable. Then

we saw there were some English. You could see where men had clawed at their faces, and throats, trying to get breath.

Some had shot themselves. The horses, still in the stables, cows, chickens, everything, all were dead. Everything, even the insects were dead.'

3. The Chemical Attack Signpost Monument

Having walked through the black entrance tunnel on your way to entering the cemetery, on the corner of the pathway you will come across a signpost pointing towards various sites around the world. Installed during the centenary of the 1915 gas attacks the signpost marks eight places where chemical weapons have been used around the world after the First World War.

The chemical weapons attack signpost. (3)

PART 3:
USEFUL
INFORMATION

Winter in the Eichenhain.

The German War Graves Commission

A brief introduction

The Volksbund Deutsche Kriegsgräberfürsorge (VDK) is a humanitarian organisation charged by the government of the Federal Republic of Germany with recording, maintaining and caring for the graves of German war casualties abroad. The Volksbund is Germany's war graves commission and provides information to relatives on all matters related to war graves. It also advises public and private institutions and promotes a culture of remembrance as well as international cooperation in the area of war grave maintenance, and encourages young people to come together to learn at the last resting places of war casualties.

The Volksbund currently has 300,000 active supporters. More than one million people take an interest in the organisation and make financial contributions. The Volksbund funds approximately two-thirds of its activities with these contributions and donations, and also with income received from legacies and bequests. The organisation also runs annual collection campaigns both door-to-door and in public spaces. Germany's regional and national government authorities provide the remainder of the funds needed.

Volksbund: an early citizens' initiative

The charity was founded on 16 December 1919 for the purpose of locating the bodies of the huge number of German soldiers who lost their lives during the First World War and to subsequently maintain their graves. The Volksbund, which saw itself as a citizens' initiative that represented the entire population, was charged with this task. By the early 1930s, the Volksbund had established numerous war cemeteries. From 1933 onwards, the Volksbund voluntarily agreed to 'Gleichschaltung' – the complete

submission and alignment to the National Socialist system of totalitarian control. During the Second World War, the war graves registration and information service of the armed forces was responsible for the establishment of military cemeteries.

The Volksbund took over these duties again from 1946 onwards, setting up over 400 war cemeteries in Germany in only a short period. In 1954, the government of the Federal Republic of Germany commissioned the Volksbund with locating, safeguarding and maintaining the graves of German war casualties abroad.

The Volksbund looks after more than 800 war cemeteries

On the basis of bilateral agreements, the Volksbund now fulfils this task in Europe and North Africa. It currently takes care of 832 war cemeteries and graves in 46 countries, the last resting places of about 2.8 million war casualties. Several thousand volunteers and 556 salaried employees now deal with the organisation's various activities.

After the political revolution in Eastern Europe, the work of the Volksbund also extended to the former Eastern Bloc countries, where around three million German soldiers lost their lives in the Second World War – almost twice as many as those resting in war cemeteries in the other European countries. This harboured huge challenges for the Volksbund: many of the more than 100,000 burial places are difficult to locate, or they have been destroyed, overbuilt or plundered.

Since 1991, the Volksbund has repaired or reconstructed 331 Second World War cemeteries and 188 burial grounds from the First World War in Eastern, Central and South-East Europe. A total of 954,146 war casualties have been reinterred in eighty-three war cemeteries.

To safeguard the work it is doing long-term, the Volksbund established the foundation 'Gedenken und Frieden' ('Peace and Remembrance') in 2001.

Combining remembrance with education

The Volksbund commemorates the casualties of war through the establishment and maintenance of war cemeteries. The vast burial grounds are a reminder of the past that also confront the living with the consequences of war and violence.

The Volksbund provides a wide range of suitable information material about the cemeteries and the issues and questions associated with war graves.

The staff charged with liaising with the relatives answer around 24,000 enquiries regarding the last resting places of casualties from both world wars every year, and help to uncover the fate of those reported as missing in action. The Volksbund also makes information about the graves of almost five million world war casualties available on its website; members of the public can now carry out a grave search online. This source of information can be accessed free of charge and is used by more than 100,000 people from all over the world every year.

In 1953, the Volksbund started to organise international youth exchanges and work camps throughout Europe under the motto 'Graveside reconciliation – peace education'.

The education officers in the regional branches collaborate with schools and higher education establishments and carry out projects in war cemeteries both in Germany and internationally.

Peace education projects throughout Europe

The four Volksbund youth exchange and education centres in the Netherlands, Belgium, France and Germany provide young people as well as adults with the perfect framework conditions for on-site peace education projects at local war cemeteries. Around 20,000 youngsters and young adults use these offers every year.

Conferences and seminars on the culture of commemoration in a European context, work camps for adults, educational trips and trips for relatives are further central pillars of the Volksbund's education work.

The Bundeswehr, the German Army, and the association of volunteer reservists support the Volksbund by providing practical help at national and international war cemeteries, during the youth exchanges organised by the Volksbund, at commemorative events and also by collecting donations both door-to-door and on the streets.

'Volkstrauertag' in November is Germany's official annual day of remembrance. The Volksbund organises the various commemorative events held throughout Germany on that day. It is an important day both in political terms and for the public; a day for mourning the dead that also serves as a reminder of how precious peace is.

The Volksbund's official patron is the President of the Federal Republic of Germany, Mr Frank-Walter Steinmeier.

Volksbund Deutsche
Kriegsgräberfürsorge e. V.
Bundesgeschäftsstelle
Abteilung Öffentlichkeitsarbeit
Referat Kommunikation
Pressesprecherin
Diane Tempel-Bornett
Tel.: 05 61–70 09–1 39
Mobil: 01 73–8 68 80 67
Sonnenallee 1
34266 Niestetal

E-Mail: presse@volksbund.de
Internet: www.volksbund.de
Spendenkonto: Commerzbank Kassel
IBAN: DE23 5204 0021 0322 2999 00
BIC: COBADEFFXXX

PILLOW STONES EXPLANATION

The pillow stones in Plots A and B, although different in size and representing differing amounts of burials, basically display the same information, that of name, rank and date of death. As you have already read some will display the letters GEF to recognize a German Jewish soldier and some will read Unbekante Soldaten (Unknown soldiers). There is one aspect of the pillow stones that is very confusing for the English-speaking visitor, that aspect being the structure and ranking system of the German Army, which is understandable when you realise that the subject is so complicated that it warrants a book of its own.

The first issue was that the German Reich did not have a common army. It was divided into the kingdom's armies of Prussia, Bavaria, Saxony and Württemberg. Despite the fact that they had similar structures and rank systems there were slight differences between the armies and in the naming of their ranks.

Secondly, the armies have been divided into infantry, cavalry and artillery, Germany then divided these three 'commands' again into different ranking systems, especially in the lowest ranks.

The soldiers of lowest rank in the infantry were called: Grenadier (grenadier), Füsilier (fusilier), Jäger (rifleman), Musketier (musketeer), Gardist (guardsman), Infanterist (infantryman), Soldat (soldier) and Pionier (engineer); this ranking depended on the units they were serving in and what their specific task

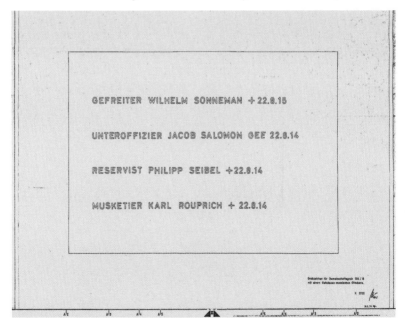

Armierungssoldat	Engineer/Bunkers
Artillerist	Gunner/Artillery
Assistenzarzt	Assistant Doctor
Bootsmannsmaat	Petty Officer/Navy
Dragoner	Dragoon/Cavalry
Einjahrigerfreiwilliger	Volunteer
Ersatz reservist	Reservist
Ersatzrekrut	Recruit
Fahnenjunker	Standard Bearer
Fahnrich	Cadet
Fahrer	Driver
Feldhilfsarzt	Field Doctor
Feldunterarzt	Field Doctor
Feldwebel	Sergeant Major
Feldwebelleutnant	Warrant Officer
Freiwilliger	Volunteer
Funker	Radio Operator
Füsilier	Rifleman
Garde – fusilier	Guardsman
Gefreiter	Lance Corporal
Gefreitet	Private
Grenadier	Grenadier
Hauptmann	Captain
Heizer	Stoker
Hornist	Bugler
Husar	Hussar
Infanterist	Infantry
Jäger	Infantry
Kanonier	Gunner/Artillery
Krankentrager	Stretcher bearer
Kriegsfreiwilliger	Volunteer
Kuassier	Cavalry
Landsturmann	Infantry
Landsturmpflichtiger	Conscript
Landsturmrekrut	Recruit
Landwehrmann	Infantry
Leutnant	2nd Lieutenant
Luftschiffer	Airship staff

Major	Major
Matrose	Sailor
Musektier	Musician
Musketier	Musketeer
Oberbootsmannsmaat	Captains mate
Oberfeldwebel	Sergeant Major
Oberfeuerwerker	Ordnance
Obergefreiter	Lance Corporal
Oberheizer	Leading Stoker
Oberjäger	Jager Corporal
Oberleutnant	Lieutenant
Obermatrose	Sailor Corporal
Offiziersanwarter	Officer Cadet
Offiziersstellvertreter	Acting Officer
Pionier	Pioneer
Rekrut	Recruit
Reservist	Reservist
Schutze	Rifleman
Seesoldat	Seaman
Sergeant	Sergeant
Signalmeister	Signaller
Soldat	Soldier
Stabsarzt	Medical Officer
Tambour	Drummer
Telefonist	Telephone Operator
Telegraphist	Telegrapher
Trainfahrer	Supply Driver
Trainreiter	Supply Cavalry
Trainsoldat	Supply man
Ulan	Cavalry
Unbekannter	Unknown
Unterarzt	Assistant Doctor
Unteroffizer	Corporal
Vizewachtmeister	Acting Sergeant
Vizfeldwebel	Acting Sergeant Major
Wachtmeister	Sergeant Major
Wehrmann	Infantry

or ability was. Thirdly it depended on what status of a soldier you have been in terms of reservists and volunteers. In the German Army you had several different levels of reservists depending upon their age and experience, they also had differences in their ranks and their reserve or volunteer status could also be combined with their rank.

To highlight the complicity of it all, David Stone wrote in his excellent book *Kaisers Army*:

'There was a military service obligation between the ages of 17 and 45. Pre-war, military service broadly followed a progression based on age. As early as 17, but more often from 18, young men would get their first introduction to military service with 2–3 years in the Landsturm (also manned by older, experienced, soldiers as we'll see). From 20–22, they moved to the active "regular" army for a 2 year stint. From there they moved to the Reserves for 4–5 years. The Reserve's role was to supplement the army on mobilisation. From the Reserves the older soldiers would serve 5 years in the first tier of the Landwehr, aged 27–35, and the second tier also for 5 years aged 33–38. In both the Reserves and first tier Landwehr they would have annual two-week refresher courses. Eventually, their final military service would be aged 39–45 in the Landsturm, meeting their younger selves starting their military service. Landsturm troops were engaged as garrison troops, POW guards, coastal defence, training units and as line of communication security.

In addition to the above, in pre-war times the available conscription exceeded the requirements of the peacetime army and navy. Some men, therefore, would be directed to the Ersatz-Reserve (where ersatz meant replacement) for a 12-year period. This functioned as a sort of reserve-reserve, where men who were physically suitable for military service but who had been exempted for family or business or economic reasons, or conceivably minor physical disabilities. After the 12 years' Ersatz-Reserve, the men would move to the second tier of the Landwehr if they had had regular training stints, or to the Landsturm if not.'

As the situation is so complicated, I have listed some of the ranks and roles featured on the pillow stones (opposite). The list is not exhaustive, but the majority is covered.

THE GERMAN JEWS OF LANGEMARK

As of the publishing date there are sixty-three German Jewish soldiers identified as being buried in Plots A and B of Langemark German cemetery with a further sixty-three commemorated on the name blocks surrounding the Kameradengrab, some of whom may be buried in the mass grave and some not. The list is by no means exhaustive as the VDK are

Plot A

Name	Grave No	Name	Grave No
Abraham, Louis	8750	Mandelbaum, Max	6281
Baruth, Walter	5174	Mandl, Georg	3976
Bodenheimer, Arthur	4842	Marx, Herbert	3937
Braunsberg, Hans	6472	Nathan, Bruno	3052
Dannenbaum, Siegmund	3899	Nimeschansky, Robert	2403
Falkson, Erich	7900	Rosenbaum, Karl	5314
Goldschmidt, Karl	2883	Schendel, Walter	1230
Golinski, Hermann	5584	Silberberg, Erich	293
Heymann, Wilhelm	2079	Speier, Adolf	7641
Jacobsohn, Arnold	6351	Stensch, Kurt	1708
Lewin, Leopold	1956	Thorner, Alfred	904
Lewy, Hermann	3419	Weinberg, Edwin	8236
Lewy, Walter	8283	Welsch, Herbert	1173
Löwenberg, Karl	4720	Werner, Nathan	3562
Löwenstern, Josef	4851	Wollstein, Siegfried	263
		Zweig, Fritz	7771

constantly searching their records to try and identify further individuals so no doubt in the future more will be added to the lists. A look at the traditional Jewish names engraved into the panels of the Listenraum will tell you that there are potentially a great many more names still to be confirmed as of the Jewish faith, Dr Kurt Salomon, is a perfect example of this.

Plot B

Name	Grave No	Name	Grave No
Adler, Ludwig	17906	Levi, Meier	10989
Altmann, Max	12509	Levy, Simon	17681
Berent, Edwin	16537	Lewin, Leo	17930
Blandovski, Max	18407	Leyens, Alfred	18994
Drucker, Saly	11519	Lion, Ernst	17741
Flatau, Leo	17757	Oppenheim, Julius	13751
Frankfurther, Fritz	15052	Orkin, Georg	19120
Goldschmidt, Hugo	11790	Rollmann, Josef Alfred	16097
Goldschmidt, Max	16290	Rosenthal, Gustav	17676
Goldstein, Arno	11618	Saalberg, Siegbert	10722
Grunewald, Ernst	12016	Sassen, Josef	13332
Hagenow, Walter	10185	Schiller, Ernst	10152
Harf, Gustav	11783	Stern, Milton	12337
Heilbronn, Max	18511	Stern, Siegfried	11387
Kaatz, Alfred	12103	Wallhausen, Siegbert	17651
Kahn, Leonhard	16724	Weinberg, Adolf	14820

Plot C: Kameradengrab

Name	Name	Name
Bauer, Ludwig	Hanauer, Willy	Nathan, Julius
Benjamin, Fritz	Herz, Adolf	Nußbaum, Ernst Salomon
Blum, Alfred	Hess, Isaak	Ottensooser, Robert
Brauer, Kurt	Hirsch, Adolf	Pollack, Eugen
Eckhaus, Jakob	Hirsch, Ernst	Reiß, Arthur
Ehrlich, Siegfried	Hirsch, Max	Ries, Arthur
Erlanger, Julius	Hirschfeld, Otto	Rosenberg, Berthold
Forchheimer, Max	Hofmann, Kurt	Rothschild, Isaak
Frank, Max	Jacobsohn, Artur	Rubel, Theobald
Frank, Otto	Joseph, Kurt	Salzmann, Kurt
Frankenstein, Arthur	Kalkstein, Erich	Schweitzer, Max
Freund, Erich	Karlsberg, Leo	Sichel, Sigmund
Freundlich, Georg	Kleeberg, Albert	Sichel, Sigmund
Geldern, Felix	Landsberger, Erich	Simon, Josef
Gerstel, Leo	Leschinski, Walter	Steinberger, Hugo
Gerstle, Isaak	Levy, Camill	Sternberg, Georg
Grausmann, David Kurt	Levy, Roger	Strauß, Adolf
Gunzenhäuser, Max	Levy, Sylvain Samuel	Strauß, Max
Halberstadt, John	Lewin, Alfred	Strauss, Moses
Hamburger, Gustav	Mantel, Siegfried	Taubenschlag, Selmar
Hamburger, Joseph	Meyer, Salomon	Vyth, Moritz

KAMERADENGRAB UNUSUAL BURIALS

As mentioned in Part Two there are several recorded 'non–standard' burials in the Kameradengrab.

Three German Nurses

Auguste Burkhardt, Margarete Ditzer and Els Hilgenberg were three German female nurses (Helferin) who died on the same day, 28/10/1918. All three were originally buried in a mass grave in Belgrade–Namur which contained in total 386 sets of German remains. The grave was exhumed in the mid–1950s and the remains were reinterred in the Kameradengrab. Once again there are conflicting accounts of how these three German nurses met their end, some sources quoting the Spanish flu whilst other sources quote 'a deadly accident'. Whatever the reason, these poor girls met an untimely end and now rest in peace possibly in Langemark.

As well as the German nurses there are a reported four Austro Hungarian soldiers, two Russian prisoners of war, one Italian prisoner of war and one Belgian civilian also recorded as being possibly interred in the Kameradengrab.

I must add a caveat to this, please remember that not all of the names mentioned on the name blocks either side of the Kameradengrab are necessarily buried there. This is true in these cases. For example in the case of the three nurses, not all the German bodies could be accounted for when the grave in Belgrade – Namur was exhumed. Belgian civilians had been buried on top of the German burials. As a result many of the Germans now recorded as being buried in Langemark from that grave (including the nurses), may still rest in what is left of the mass grave in Belgrade – Namur.

LANGEMARK KEY POINTS IN HISTORY

1914 Creation of cemetery

1918 Armistice

1919 Treaty of Versaille makes Belgium responsible for war graves within its borders

1926 Belgium and German War Graves Agreement hands over control of the cemeteries to the Germans

1932 Cemetery inauguration. 10,143 burials. Cemetery becomes a focus for German youth groups

May 1940 Germany invades Belgium. Demands that Belgium pays for the upkeep of German cemeteries within its borders.

June 1940 Hitler visits Langemark for propaganda purposes

1944 Germans leave Belgium

1954 Belgium German War Graves Agreement. Germany pays compensation and takes over control of Langemark

1955–7 Concentration of burials into the cemetery leading to burials in Plot B and creation of Kameradengrab and installation of Emil Krieger's statues. c.44,000 burials in cemetery

1959 cemetery designer Robert Tischler dies

1960 New designer Georg Fischbacher

1970s redesign. Pillow stones installed, some basalt crosses removed and oak trees thinned out

1983 Eighty-four name blocks around Kameradengrab installed, wall demolished and statues moved to rear of cemetery

2006 Car park and entrance tunnel built

2015 Major cemetery renovation, wall rebuilt and statues moved back to original position

LANGEMARK MYTHS AND URBAN LEGENDS

As a well-established tour guide in the Ypres Salient I have visited the German cemetery in Langemark many times over the past decade. Although the sites we visit pretty much remain the same, each tour is different due to to the wide social mix of clients we accompany around the Salient. Clients come to this area from all over the world, many have direct links to the area having relatives buried or commemorated here and some come purely from a historical interest and to pay their respects to a generation now passed. No matter what their nationality or reasons for visiting nearly every visitor is taken aback by the scale of burials at Langemark, its atmosphere and its general level of upkeep. I always look forward to our stop at Langemark as it generates many questions and comments. Time has proven to be a great healer and so it is very rare to receive negative comments about the German soldier of the First World War from our clients, hand on heart I can say I have only had one bad experience from a client in the last ten years or so. The questions asked always tend to be the same ones, mainly 'Do you get many Germans visit?' or 'What do the locals think of the Germans?', from time to time, however, a more unusual question or comment will surface mainly as a result of myths and local legends that surround the cemetery, some generated by the anti-German feeling here at the end of the Second World War and some because of the lack of material published of the history of the cemetery. I have listed some of the more common questions asked to me and my colleagues and a response in an attempt to clarify these issues.

1. 'Is this where they are all buried standing up?'

This is a myth. In Plots A and B there are allotted grave plots, some plots have multiple occupancy ie double-stacked but they are definitely laid flat. The remains in the Kameradengrab are stacked on top of each other and also lay flat.

2. 'The cemetery looks unkept, the Germans don't care about their war dead.'

As you have read earlier a great deal of thought has gone into the design of the cemetery taking into account the German design principles of the time which differed greatly from the British design principles. The Germans do care about their war dead and as time passes feel more able to visit these sites. A lack of state funding of the Volksbund Deutsche Kriegsgräberfürsorge (VDK) means that they cannot have the same level of upkeep we see in British and Commonwealth cemeteries, there are no full-time gardeners here employed by the VDK, instead local contactors are used when the grass gets too long or leaves need sweeping. Once every two years or so volunteers from the German armed forces or student groups come to the cemetery to clean the pillow stones and rewhiten the names.

3. 'There are no upright grave markers as the Belgium government would not allow it.'

I believe this to be a locally generated myth. It was the Germans decision to remove the upright wooden grave crosses in the mid 1950s due to their poor state of repair.

4. 'Is the mass grave a burial pit?'
No. The Kameradengrab is a purpose-built ossuary constructed from reinforced concrete which was then sealed on completion.

5. 'The names on the blocks surrounding the mass grave are the names of men who were later identified as being buried there.'
This is incorrect, the names on the blocks surrounding the Kameradengrab are nearly (but not exclusively) names sourced from Bavarian records of all Bavarian soldiers missing in Belgium in the First World War, some may be interred in the Kameradengrab and some will not. The archives from Prussia, Saxony and Wurtemburg did not survive the Second World War so there is no way of working out the figures for their missing. If it helps think of the blocks as a 'Menin Gate' type memorial for the Bavarians plus a few additions.

6. 'The German flying ace Werner Voss is buried in the Kameradengrab.'
The remains of Werner Voss were never recovered, his original grave was destroyed in the fighting of 1917. Voss is one of the exceptions to the rule mentioned in the previous answer, although he was a Prussian his name is commemorated on the name blocks either as a result of family request or by the fact that he was a 'personality' who was known to be missing in the area.

7. 'Are there non-German nationals buried in the Kamerangrab?'
Yes, there are two British soldiers in the Kameradengrab plus at least one Belgian national that we know of. It is very possible there may be more but we will never know for sure.

8. 'The names carved into the oak panels in the Listenraum are all names of the German student soldiers killed in 1914.'
This is incorrect. Historians put a figure of circa 3,000 soldiers of the so-called student regiments being killed during the Kindermord and there are over 6,000 names carved into the panels. The names on the panels are the names of the identified burials in Plot A of the cemetery on its inauguration in 1932.

9. 'The names on the oak panels are the names of the unidentified soldiers buried in Plot A'.
Again incorrect, see answer above.

10. 'Hitler wanted all references to Jewish Soldiers removed from Langemark.'
Possibly is the answer. There is documented evidence that German Jewish grave markers were removed in France (Cambrai for example) and then remarked as unidentified soldiers. Langemark is a different case though as all the grave markers at the time were crosses and marked by serial numbers as opposed to names. The only visual evidence of German Jewish names are those carved into the oak panels in the Listenraum and they still remain to this day.

11. 'The German bunkers in Plot B are not original and were purpose built for the cemetery.'
The bunkers in Plot B ARE original but they were restored in the 1930s. Plans drawn up at the time by the VDK show the original bunkers and the restoration work that was to take place.

12. 'The bunkers are sinking into the ground.'
If you look at the rear of the bunkers you can see that the entrances are

partly below ground level. The reason for this though is not because they are sinking it is because there would have been a trench connecting the bunkers and so access into them was via the trench (which is below ground level) and through the bunker doorway. The aforementioned bunker plans also shows the bunker dimensions including below ground, therefore I believe they are not sinking.

13. 'The blocks between the bunkers are anti-tank defences.'

This is incorrect, the blocks were foreseen to be constructed on the original design plans of the cemetery from the 1930s, and were originally planned as a design feature to represent the German front line as it winds its way across Flanders. Granite name blocks were attached to the main concrete block to recognise the regiments and student associations who funded the cemetery.

14. 'Do many Germans visit the cemetery?'

No is the straight answer, however the cemetery is very well visited by guests from other nations, in fact it is the third biggest visitor 'attraction' in the area after Tyne Cot cemetery and the In Flanders Fields Museum, attracting 1.1 million visitors at the height of the centenary in 2018.

15. 'The Treaty of Versailles stipulated that the wooden crosses in German cemeteries were to be painted black as the Germans were the guilty party.'

Myth. There is no mention of this in the Treaty of Versailles. The German crosses were black due to the wood preservative used to protect them from the elements.

GLOSSARY OF TERMS

ADG: Amtliche Deutsche Gräberdienst

Buche Allee: Beech Alley

CWGC: Commonwealth War Graves Commission

Ehrenfeld: Field of Honour

Ehrenhalle: Hall of Honour

Ehrenhof: Courtyard of Honour

Ehrenraum: Room of Honour

Eichenhain: Oak Grove

IWGC: Imperial War Graves Commission

Kameradengrab: Comrades Grave

Listenraum: List Room

Listraum: List Room

Mohnfeld: Poppy Field

NSDAP: Nationalsozialistische Deutsche Arbeiterpartei

Soldatenfriedhof: Soldiers cemetery

Studentenfriedhof: Student cemetery

VDK: Volksbund Deutsche Kriegsgräberfürsorge

Vorplatz: Forecourt

Vorraum: Vestibule

Wassergraben: Moat

Weiheraum: Sacred Room

ACKNOWLEDGEMENTS AND CREDITS

Barron, Rosemary, Casualty and Compassionate Centre:
  Research

Bayerische Staatsbibliothek München/Bildarchiv:
  Historical Photography

Burrows, Ilka, Volksbund Deutsche
  Kriegsgräberfürsorge e.v, Kassel: Research

Connelly Professor, Mark: Historical Photography

D'Hondt, Jan, Westtoer: Photography

Debaeke, S.: Historical Photography

Deraeve W.: Historical Photography

Degraeve, Roland: Photography

Douglas, S.: Photography

Gearing, Ryan: Photography

Goebel, Stefan: Historical Photography

Greet, Michael, Commonwealth War Graves
  Commission: Research

In Flanders Fields Museum: Historical Images

Mahieu, P.: Photography

Page, J.: Photography

Passler, P., Volksbund Deutsche Kriegsgräberfürsorge
  e.v, Kassel: Historical Photography

Passler, P., Volksbund Deutsche Kriegsgräberfürsorge
  e.v, Kassel: Plans and Maps

Profi, M.: Photography

Schock, T., Volksbund Deutsche Kriegsgräberfürsorge
  e.v, Kassel: Research

Steward, R.: Photography

Stichelbault, B.: Aerial Photography

Taghon, Peter: Historical Photography

Verdeghem, S., Archeologist, Skylarcs: Research

Thanks to the Volksbund Deutsche Kriegsgräberfürsorge
(VDK) for their invaluable help and considerable time
given in the compiling of this publication.

BIBLIOGRAPHY AND FURTHER READING

Beckett, I., Ypres. 1st Battle 1914. (2006) Routledge

Berliner Illustrierte Nachtausgabe 9/7/32

Connelly, M., Goebel S. Ypres. (2018) Oxford University Press

Convention: belgo – allemande du–6–mars – 1926

Convention: verbale – relative – aux – cimetieres – franco – allemandes – Luxembourg – belge 1934

Dendooven, D., (2014) Menin Gate and Last Post. De Klaproos Editions

Deutsche: belgisches kriegsgräberabkommem 28/5/54

Deutsche: belgisches kriegsgräberabkommem 8/7/54

Deutsche Kriegeräber und denkmäler in Belgien 23/8/27, Deutsche gefandschaft Brüssel

Deutsche Kriegergräber aus den Weltkriege 1914/1918

Deutsche Kriegsgräberabkommem 10/3/52 VDK

Erlaeuterungsbericht: 1929 friedhof Langemark

Freiburger Tagblatt no 263 November 12th 1914

Freytag, A. and Driessche, T., (2011) Die Deutschen Soldatenfriedhof des Ersten Weltkriegs in Flandern

www.germancemeteriesofthegreatwarinbelgium.wordpress.com

Graham, S., The Challenge of the Dead. (1921) Cassell and Company Ltd

Holt, Tonie and Vamai. (2011) Ypres Salient and Passchendaele. Pen and Sword Military

Howe, H., Missinne, R.,Verbeke, R. De Duitse, begraafplaats in Langemark. (2011) De Klaproos

In Flanders Fields Museum Research Centre, Ypres Belgium

Juda in Langemark. (1933) Weltbuehne

Juedische Grabstele 1418. Volksbund Deutsche Kriegsgräberfürsorge e.v, Kassel

Keith, A.W., From Ypres to Amiens 1938. The Citizen July 23rd 1938

Kriegsgräberfürsorge. (1933) Volksbund Deutsche
Kriegsgräberfürsorge e.v, Kassel

Kriegsgräberfürsorge. (1940) Volksbund Deutsche
Kriegsgräberfürsorge e.v, Kassel

Lafarge Philippe. Cambrai Le Cimetiere Militaire de la Route
de Solesmes

Leroy T, Kremer A, Plomion. Oak Tree Symbolism in the
Light of Genomics

Mortimer G Davidson. Kunst in Deutschland 1933–1945
Architektur. Grabert

Mortimer G Davidson. Kunst in Deutschland 1933–1945
Skulpturen. Grabert

Niederschrift über die sitzung des kunstausschusses 17/12/29

Stichelbault B, Chielens P. The Great War Seen From the Air
(2013) Mercatorfonds, Brussels

Stone, D. Kaisers Army (2015) Bloomsbury

Vancoillie, J. 'From Field Grave to Comrades' Grave. The
German First World War Graves on the Flanders Front',
RIHA Journal 0162, 27 June 2017

Verstraete, P. Soldatenfriedhof Langemarck. (2009) Kortrijk
Groeninghe

www.yprespeacemonument.com

Zentralnachweiseamt für Kriegerverluste und Kriegergräber,
Berlin 16/1/39

Ypres Battlefield Tours

www.ypresbattlefieldtours.be